Fighting Napoleon's Empire

Fighting Napoleon's Empire

The Campaigns of a British Infantryman in Italy, Egypt, the Peninsular & the West Indies During the Napoleonic Wars

Joseph Anderson

Including
A Brief History of Joseph Anderson's Campaigns
by Eric Sheppard

Fighting Napoleon's Empire: The Campaigns of a British Infantryman in Italy, Egypt, the Peninsular & the West Indies During the Napoleonic Wars
by Joseph Anderson

Including *A Brief History of Anderson's Campaigns*
by Eric Sheppard

First published in 1913 in
Recollections of a Peninsular Veteran

A Brief History of Joseph Anderson's Campaigns by Eric Sheppard
has been adapted by the Leonaur editors from
A Short History of the British Army to 1914
first published in 1926

FIRST EDITION

Published by Leonaur Ltd

Copyright in this form © 2007 Leonaur Ltd

ISBN (10 digit): 1-84677-143-9 (hardcover)
ISBN (13 digit): 978-1-84677-143-9 (hardcover)

ISBN (10 digit): 1-84677-141-2 (softcover)
ISBN (13 digit): 978-1-84677-141-5 (softcover)

http://www.leonaur.com

Publisher's Notes

In the interests of authenticity, the spellings, grammar and place names used have been retained from the original editions.

The opinions of the authors represent a view of events in which he was a participant related from his own perspective, as such the text is relevant as an historical document.

The views expressed in this book are not necessarily those of the publisher.

Contents

Introduction	7
Early Experiences	9
The Campaign of Maida	16
In Egypt	21
The El-Hamet Disaster	26
The Battle of Talavera	31
The Battle of Busaco	37
The Lines of Torres Vedras	43
The Lost Regimental Books	48
The Battle of Fuentes D'Onoro	53
In Scotland	59
Voyage to Barbados	63
St. Vincent and Guadeloupe	71
Dominica	77
An Amusing Duel	82
Chased by a Pirate	88
Life in Jamaica	96
Home Again and Married	102
To New South Wales	109

A Brief History of Joseph Anderson's Campaigns

Publisher's Note	113
The Campaign in Egypt	115
The Italian Campaign	118
The Peninsular War	122
The West Indies	153

Introduction

The following pages have been selected from the autobiography of my grandfather, the late Colonel Joseph Anderson, who was born in Sutherlandshire, Scotland, on June 1, 1790, and died on July 18, 1877. It should be stated that this narrative was written only for his own family. He had never kept a diary—nor even any notes of his adventures and travels—and only began to write his reminiscences of the long-past years when he was seventy-four, in the quiet of his beautiful home near Melbourne, Australia. His memory was perfectly amazing; but if any slight inaccuracies should be discovered, the reader is asked to excuse them, on account of his age. He was a "grand old man" in every sense, and lived in excellent health of mind and body until his eighty-eighth year. To the very last he was always keenly interested in military matters, and never failed to attend, in uniform, all the important volunteer reviews held in Melbourne, where his upright, soldierly figure attracted universal admiration. His son, the late Colonel Acland Anderson, C.M.G., was for many years the Colonel-Commandant of the Military Forces of H.M. Government in Victoria, which appointment he held till his death in January, 1882. He was the founder of the Volunteer Organization, as in 1855 he raised a Rifle Corps in Melbourne, which was not only the first in Victoria but probably the first in Australia.

Acland Anderson

Chapter 1
Early Experiences

I suddenly and most unexpectedly got my commission as an ensign in the 78th Regiment (27th June, 1805) through the influence of my brother William, a captain in the same corps, being then only within a few days of my fifteenth year.

But before I go any further I must mention an amusing incident which took place before I left Banff Academy to join my regiment, and as in the present day it may not appear much to my credit, I beg my dear ones who may read this to remember I was still a boy, and with less experience of the world than most of the youths of the present day.

Out of my pocket money I managed to save six shillings, with which I purchased an old gun to amuse myself, and to shoot sparrows during our play hours; and this being contrary to all rules and positive standing orders, I kept my dangerous weapon at an old woman's house a little way from town. A few chosen companions knew of my secret and accompanied me one evening to enjoy our sport, but there was one amongst them to whom I refused a shot, so next day he reported me and my gun to the second master. I was called up and questioned on his evidence, when I stoutly and boldly denied every word he said. The good master, Mr. Simpson, then said, "You have told a lie, sir, and I must punish you; so down with your breeches."

I at once resisted, and said, "I am an officer and won't submit."

He then called two or three boys to assist him in clearing for action, but I still resisted, and kicked and thumped them all round, until the noise became so loud that the good old rector came in from his room and said, "What is all this?"

On his being told, and also my reasons for resisting, he laughed most heartily and said, "I will not disgrace you, sir; you are an officer, and I will not disgrace you."

So I was allowed to escape and to go back to my seat. Many years afterwards I returned to Banff, and the rector and I had many laughs over this frolic, and at the same time I met Mr. Simpson, but found it difficult to convince him of my continued good will, and that I never forgot the good and salutary lesson he gave me.

Six weeks after this I received a letter from my brother ordering me to join my regiment, then stationed at Shorncliffe barracks in Kent, and directing me at the same time to go in the first instance to my uncle, Dr. Anderson, at Peterhead, to receive an outfit, and then, without being allowed to go home to see my father, I was shipped off for London in one of the trading sloops of that day, and consigned to another friend of ours, Mr. Tod, who was married to my only aunt. They received me most kindly, and here I found a number of young ladies, my cousins, who were about my own age, and with whom I soon became happy and intimate. I remained with them for a fortnight, and during that time Mr. Tod took me to his tailor, who furnished me with all my necessary regimentals, and not a little proud was I on finding myself for the first time dressed out in scarlet and gold. Mr. Tod took me also to many of the public places and streets of London, and to this day I cannot forget how the good old man laughed at my surprise and remarks about all the pretty women who unblushingly stared at me.

On the 18th August, 1805, I took my leave, and by coach proceeded to join my regiment at Shorncliffe barracks. My brother William received me on my arrival, and then took me to the colonel to introduce me, and afterwards to the adjutant to report my arrival, and then to my future home for a time, his own house at Sandgate; and with him I remained for two months, until we marched for Portsmouth to embark for Gibraltar. In the meantime I attended all daily parades, morning and evening, and was drilled and instructed in a squad with the men.

But before I go any further I must mention that soon after joining the regiment my brother told me I was never regularly gazetted to my ensigncy. That appointment had been given to my brother John, who at the same time got a cadetship in the Madras Army, which my father considered the best appointment of the two, and consequently wrote to my brother William to use his interest with General McKenzie Fraser, the full colonel of the 78th (from whom the ensigncy was procured), to say that his brother John was provided for, but that he had another brother, Joseph, to whom he hoped he would kindly transfer the commission; and this the general at once consented to do, and so I was ordered to join, and for nearly two years after my name appeared "John Anderson" in the Army List. Such chances do not happen nowadays.

We arrived at Portsmouth at the beginning of October, and embarked on the following day for Gibraltar. The transports of those days were wretched, and their provisions were even worse, and in the miserable tub *Neptune*, to which I was doomed, we were so crowded that I, as the youngest subaltern, had neither berth nor cot allowed me, and I was obliged to double up with another young ensign, and to make the best I could of it. Yet we were very jolly, and all went on well until we got off Lisbon, about the 19th of October, when the commodore of all the other ships-of-war in charge of the convoy made the signal, "An enemy in sight, put in to port in view," and this was immediately answered by every ship in the convoy.

The whole fleet then went about and steered direct for Lisbon, and so we continued with every sail set, until on the same evening, and following day, we were all safely at anchor in the Tagus. We heard soon after, that the enemy we discovered in time was part of the French fleet then making for Trafalgar, and in a few days more we had the great and glorious news of Nelson's splendid and complete victory over the combined fleets of France and Spain off Cape Trafalgar, on the 21st October, 1805, and of their almost complete capture and destruction. But, alas! how great was the price of this national success, for Nelson fell, and many gallant officers, soldiers, and sailors with him.

A few days after receiving this great news we again sailed from Lisbon for Gibraltar, and beyond Cape Trafalgar we came up with our own partly dismasted and disabled ships, and all which could be safely brought away of the enemy's captured vessels, the former proudly distinguished by their English tattered flags, and the latter humbled by the British ensign flying triumphantly over the national emblems of France and Spain. This was indeed a proud sight, and a lasting day of triumph and renown to old England, for from that time to the present hour the might of the Spanish navy was crushed and the French navy never appeared formidable to us again. We soon passed our noble heroes and their prizes, and our fleet reached Gibraltar a few days afterwards.

The regiment landed next day, and occupied Windmill Hill and Europa Point barracks. There were no less than four other regiments there when we arrived, and I liked that gay station very much. But there for the first and only time of my military life I was put in arrest, and became so alarmed that I cried bitterly, and thought I was going to be hanged at least!

The other ensigns of the regiment were all many years older than I, and one of them in particular used to bully and annoy me constantly, so that on one of these occasions I made use of most insulting and un-gentlemanlike language to him. Our kind and parental colonel (Macleod of Guinnes) was then in the habit of inviting all the young officers to breakfast with him, and on the following morning I went as usual in full dress to his house, about a mile from our barracks, and there on entering I found Cameron seated with others. The colonel soon appeared, and wished all good morning in his accustomed kind manner and asked us to take our seats. Breakfast passed over as usual. As soon as the table was cleared Colonel Macleod stood up and called us all to him, and then, addressing me, said, "Mr. Anderson, Mr. Cameron has reported to me that you have been making use of most improper language to him, and as you seem to forget you are no longer a schoolboy, but an officer, I must put you under arrest, and send you home in disgrace to your family. Leave your sword there, sir [on the table], and go to your barracks immediately." Poor me! I at once showed I was still but a schoolboy, for I cried and sobbed fearfully, and returned to my barracks with a broken heart.

The same evening a dear friend of my family, Captain John Mackay of Bighouse, called on me (no doubt at the request of the colonel), and frightened me more than ever, for he told me again that I would be brought to a general court-martial and deprived of my commission. I now cried more than ever, and I told him all that had passed between me and Cameron, and the constant insults and liberties he attempted to take with me in the presence of the other officers. I was glad to see from my friend's remarks that he began to think Cameron was more to blame than I was, yet he still told me I must prepare for the worst, and so he left me to my own misery. I shall never forget my sufferings that night. However, next day I was ordered to attend at the colonel's quarters, and there found most of the officers assembled, Cameron amongst them.

The colonel then addressed us, and said, "Mr. Anderson, I have been inquiring into your conduct, and find that you, Mr. Cameron, most grossly insulted this young gentleman, and by your daring, unwarrantable, and most un-officerlike conduct provoked a young boy to forget himself. You, sir, are many years older and ought to know better; I consider you therefore far more culpable and blameable in every respect than Mr. Anderson. You have both acted very improperly, but for the present I shall take no further notice of your conduct than with this reprimand to warn you both to be more careful and correct for the future; and now, Mr. Anderson, you are released from your arrest, and will return to your duty."

Off I went in joy to my barracks, thankful indeed for this proper support and friendly admonition, and from that day I enjoyed myself and felt happy with my brother officers.

I was at this time attached to a company commanded by an old and experienced officer, Lieutenant James Mackay, a most studious man, and an acknowledged scholar, whose pride, next to his profession, was in his books. His instruction and care did me more good than any previous or subsequent opportunities I ever had for study. I was quartered with him at Europa Point, and he made me rise early and visit our men's barracks at Windmill Hill, two miles distant, every morning. I then returned to breakfast with him, after which we went to our public parade, which was no sooner over than we got home, and then he made me sit down to certain books and studies which he gave me. This he made me continue daily while we remained at Gibraltar, although (at the instigation of the other officers) I often tricked him, and tried hard to get off from such control and (as I then thought) drudgery.

Being a perfect master of the French language, he was one of the British officers sent with Napoleon Bonaparte to the island of St. Helena, and afterwards recalled by our Government on the suspicion of being too intimate with the ex-Emperor.

Chapter 2

The Campaign of Maida

Early in 1806 our regiment left Gibraltar for Messina, where we continued some months, and then marched for Messina, where we camped until we embarked, in June of the same year, as a part of the expedition under Lieut.-General Sir John Stuart for Calabria, landing with the other troops in the gulf of St. Euphemia on the morning of the 1st of July.

The object of this force was to attack the French General Regnier, then in that part of Italy with a considerable army. Our landing was but slightly opposed, because our convoy, the *Endymion* frigate (Captain Hoste), took up her position as near the shore as possible, and by her fire soon cleared the beach and drove the enemy far beyond our first footing. He made a partial stand, however, on a rising ground inland; but as our troops advanced, and after a skirmish, we soon forced him to retreat on his supports and finally on his main body. We then halted for the day, and the enemy left advanced posts and videttes to watch our movements. We soon bivouacked for the night about 6 miles from the beach, with, of course, the same precautions. During that evening and the following day we were busily engaged in landing our heavy stores of provisions.

On the 3rd July we advanced a few miles to reconnoitre and to gain information of the enemy's force and main position, and on the memorable and beautiful morning of the 4th July we finally advanced in columns, and soon found ourselves on the unusually clear and extensive plain of Maida, the enemy showing in mass on the distant hills and woods, about three miles from us, with a river in front which greatly strengthened their position.

As soon as we got half across the plain, our columns were halted, and the troops deployed into two lines, the one to support the other, with our skirmishers thrown out in front to cover us. We were then directed to "order arms and stand at ease"; thus formed, we offered a fair field to the enemy. Our brigade, consisting of the 58th, 78th, and 81st Regiments, under General Acland, formed our front line, and in this position we remained at least half an hour gazing at our enemy; by this time the French were seen in full view debouching from the hills and woods, and, crossing the river, they advanced with all confidence towards us. As soon as they had cleared the river their advance halted, and the whole then formed into two columns, in which order they steadily advanced with drums playing and colours flying. We remained quiet and steady, but impatient, on our ground, and had a full view of our foes, as they boldly and confidently advanced, evidently expecting that they could, and would, walk over us; and so they ought to have done, for we afterwards ascertained they numbered upwards of nine thousand of their best troops, while our force did not much exceed six thousand men! Their cavalry was also more numerous, for we had only one squadron of the 23rd Light Dragoons; but ours was so admirably managed that it kept the others in check during the whole day.

As soon as these formidable French columns came sufficiently near, and not till then, our lines were called to "attention" and ordered to "shoulder arms." Then commenced in earnest the glorious battle of Maida, first with a volley from our brigade into the enemy's columns and from our artillery at each flank without ceasing, followed by independent file firing as fast as our men could load; and well they did their work! Nor were the enemy idle; they returned our fire without ceasing, then in part commenced to deploy into line. The independent file firing was still continued with more vigour than ever for at least a quarter of an hour, when many brave men fell on both sides. Our brigade was then ordered to charge, supported by our second line, and this they did lustily and with endless hearty cheers, the French at the same moment following our example and advancing towards us at a steady charge of bayonets, the rolling of drums, and endless loud cheers. Both armies were equally determined to carry all before them; it was not till we got within five or six paces of each other that the enemy wavered, broke their ranks, and gave way, turning away to a man and scampering off, most of them throwing away their arms at the same time; but our men continued their cheers and got up with some of them, and numbers were either bayoneted, shot, or taken prisoners. The enemy was then fairly driven over the bridge by which they had advanced, or forced into the river, where numbers were captured or drowned.

Our loss was comparatively small. The brave 78th had about a dozen men killed and many wounded. The 20th Regiment landed during the action, and by an able and hurried manoeuvre managed to get on the enemy's right flank, and contributed much to the success of the day. Captain McLean, of that regiment, was the only officer killed in the battle. I shall never forget my horror when I beheld numbers of gallant French soldiers weltering in their blood and groaning in agony from the most fearful wounds. And here I must mention an incident to the honour and credit of one of our Highland sergeants of grenadiers, Farquhar McCrae, who could not speak one word of English nor of French. He was wounded after we had passed over the first line of dead and dying Frenchmen, and while passing through the heap of wounded one of them made him a sign that he wanted a drink, on which McCrae immediately turned round and made towards the river; but he had no sooner done so, than his ungrateful enemy levelled his musket and wounded him slightly in the arm. McCrae looked back, saw from whom the shot came, and going up to the man he seized his firelock, and after a struggle soon got it away from him; then, taking it by the muzzle, raised the butt over the Frenchman's head and said, with a terrible Gaelic oath, "I'll knock your brains out!" But a more generous impulse seized him; he actually went back to the river and brought the wretched man some water!

I have heard that in Lieut.-General Sir John Stewart's official dispatch concerning the battle of Maida it is stated that the bayonets of the contending forces actually crossed during the charge. They may have done so, in some parts of the line—but so far as I could see they did not do so, and I have never heard any one who was in the action say that "the bayonets actually crossed."

The defeat was perfect, and the victory glorious beyond all praise. We remained on the field of battle burying our dead and attending the wounded and embarking our prisoners; then we marched for Reggio, the castle of which was then besieged by some others of our troops from Sicily, who now joined our force, except the 78th Regiment, which was at once embarked under convoy of the *Endymion* frigate and destined for the capture of the fortress of Catrone, on the east coast of Italy. We arrived and anchored off that place.

About a week afterwards the *Endymion* took up her position within range of the fort, and all were ordered to be in readiness for an immediate landing. Major Macdonnell was sent on shore with a flag of truce and proposals to the governor of the fort to surrender. He returned to say that the terms were accepted. Some companies of the 78th were then landed near the fort, when the whole French garrison marched out as prisoners of war and laid down their arms in front of our line, being allowed to retain only their personal baggage, and the officers their swords. They were at once embarked and divided amongst our transports. The fort was dismantled and the guns spiked. We re-embarked, and our little fleet sailed in triumph back to Messina; but on landing we were ordered to Syracuse, and sent detachments to Augusta and to Taormina. I was with the latter, and had not been long there before I fancied myself in love with the daughter of a widow, who did all she could to encourage me and tempt me to a marriage by constantly parading a quantity of silver plate and jewels as a part of my portion; but this chance of my imaginary good luck was soon put an end to, for I was suddenly called back to headquarters, Syracuse, and there forgot my love affair.

Chapter 3

In Egypt

In March, 1807, we embarked as part of an expedition from Sicily under General McKenzie Fraser, destined for Egypt. We sailed from Syracuse on the 7th, arrived at Aboukir Bay about the middle of the same month, and found there a large fleet of our men-of-war and a numerous fleet of transports with the other troops of our expedition. The object of our force was to create a diversion in favour of Russia against the Turkish army in that country.

On the following morning all our light men-of-war and gunboats took up their stations as near the landing-place as the depth of the water would permit. The first division of our troops were at the same time ordered into the different ships' launches and towed by the smaller boats to the shore, a distance of at least four miles; but the weather was unusually fine. A considerable body of the enemy appeared on the sand-hill above the landing-place, but our gun-brig and gunboats soon dispersed them, and we landed without difficulty, except a good wetting as far as the knee, for the water was shallow and our boats could not get nearer than a few yards from the beach. The remainder of the troops followed in the course of the day, and landed with the same success and safety, and next morning the stores, camp equipage, and guns were landed without accident. The usual advance-guard was pushed forward, and the remainder of the troops followed in divisions, the enemy's advanced posts retiring before us, and that evening we camped, without any covering, on the dry sand, about six miles inland. Some of the enemy's cavalry were visible, but only in small numbers to watch our movements.

Next day we commenced our march for Alexandria, with very little interruption, beyond occasionally seeing large detachments of Turkish cavalry, with which our advanced guards and videttes exchanged shots and some volleys occasionally. Our advance to Alexandria continued much in the same way for a few days; we had fine weather and hot sands for our beds, with which we covered ourselves over. We felt well and slept very comfortably, and it was not till we arrived before the walls of the town that the enemy appeared in force and attempted to dispute our advance, but after a partial action and the loss of a few men killed and wounded we soon drove them before us and forced them to take shelter behind the walls of the town, and soon after the firing ceased on both sides for that day. We camped as before, beyond the walls of the old town, with our advanced piquets posted, and all other necessary precautions. It was found next morning that the enemy had evacuated the city of Alexandria during the night, and we then took formal possession, keeping most of our troops still in camp.

A force of about twelve hundred men was now told off and detached under Brigadier-General Wauchope to proceed against the town of Rosetta, on the Nile. They arrived before that place in twelve days, in safety. The general marched his men right into the centre of the town without any opposition, not even seeing an enemy, but then, being entrapped, a heavy fire was opened upon him from the tops of the houses and windows, without even the power of returning a shot. Death and confusion followed. General Wauchope was amongst the first who fell dead, and in a few minutes nearly all his detachment were either killed or wounded, and those who escaped for the moment were made prisoners and with the wounded put to death, so that only a few escaped altogether, and these found their way back to Alexandria to tell the sad and murderous tale.

This barbarous and butchering defeat required to be avenged, and a second force of about eighteen hundred men, under Major-General Sir W. Stewart, was told off for this service, in which my regiment, the 78th, was included.

We marched from Alexandria late in March and arrived before Rosetta on the 7th of April, and on getting into position before the town the first thing we saw was the dead and mutilated bodies of hundreds of the former force. They were, of course, at once buried, and vengeance was the prevailing cry and feeling of the living.

The late Field-Marshal Sir John Burgoyne was then a captain and our chief engineer. He at once began to throw up breastworks and other temporary defences for our guns and for the troops, these being partly completed by the next day. Some of our heavy ordnance were in battery, and commenced at once to shell the town; at the same time the enemy opened a heavy fire of artillery upon us, which was continued by both sides until dark.

Rosetta is a walled town, known then to be strongly fortified. Our works were continued day and night, and additional guns got into position, until all were mounted and brought to bear on the town. The only visible good effect our cannonade produced was the cutting in two and upsetting of many lofty minarets of the mosques; we never heard the extent of their losses, but as Rosetta was full of troops and inhabitants, their casualties must have been very considerable. All our efforts failed to make any practicable breach in the walls, therefore no regular assault was attempted. Almost every evening the enemy sallied forth in large detachments of cavalry and infantry to attack our advance posts and picquets, but our troops of dragoons (ever on the watch) soon met them, and generally dispersed them; but they never gave us a fair chance, for they usually galloped off and got back to their stronghold just as we had an opportunity of destroying them.

Ten days after we commenced this siege, our good, gallant Colonel McLeod, of the 78th, was detached with five hundred men for El-Hamet, some 50 miles higher up the Nile, to check any reinforcements or surprise by additional troops coming down the Nile from Cairo to Rosetta, and our own main body continued the siege much in the same daily routine for a fortnight longer, but still unfortunately without any success in making a practicable breach in the outer walls so as to give us a fair chance of assault. All this time we were losing many brave men. It was then finally determined to raise the siege as hopeless, and to return to Alexandria. Orders to this effect were sent to Colonel McLeod, with instructions to meet us on a given day and hour at Lake Etcho; therefore, during the night of the 20th of April our batteries were dismantled and all our heavy guns spiked and buried deeply in the sand.

On the morning of the 21st our troops were under arms and formed into a hollow square, with a few pieces of light artillery and ammunition and stores in the centre. In this way we commenced our retreat for Lake Etcho. We had scarcely moved off when our square was surrounded by thousands of Turkish cavalry and infantry, howling, screaming, and galloping like savages around us, at the same time firing at us from their long muskets, but fortunately with comparatively little loss to us. We occasionally halted our square, wheeled back a section, and gave them a few rounds of shot and shell from our artillery, then moved on in the same good order. This was a long and trying day, and the only retreat in square I ever saw. It occupied us nearly twelve hours, from five in the morning till the same hour in the evening. The enemy, with fearful shouts, followed us, firing the while of that time, but they never showed any positive determination to charge or to break our square. We were not so delicate with them, for we gave them many rounds from our guns, and when they ventured sufficiently near they were sure of more volleys than one, and we had the satisfaction of seeing numbers of them fall. We had few men killed, who were unavoidably left behind, but we were able to carry away our wounded.

CHAPTER 4

The El-Hamet Disaster

We had soon another trial awaiting us. When we got to Etcho there was no appearance of Colonel McLeod or his detachment, nor any message from him. It was therefore at once determined to march back to El-Hamet, to ascertain his fate; and there we received information that Colonel McLeod had been attacked that morning by a large force of Turks in boats from Cairo, and the whole of his detachment destroyed, and he, that good and promising soldier, was amongst the first who fell. After a short council of war we again wheeled about and marched back to Etcho, where we camped for the night. Next day we continued our retreat to Alexandria, where we arrived without any further molestation.

Day by day several rumours reached us about our lost detachment and the gallant defence they made, but nothing positive or upon which we could rely, until the sudden appearance, six weeks afterwards, at Alexandria of Lieutenant Mathieson, who was one of the survivors, who now came to us in a Turkish dress with some proposals from the Turks at Cairo. From him we learnt that they were attacked most unexpectedly on the morning of the 21st April by a large Turkish force, who came down the Nile in boats from Cairo, on their way to Rosetta, and after gallantly resisting until more than two-thirds of their number were either killed or wounded, and the last rounds of ammunition expended, the remnant were overpowered and obliged to surrender. He also described their position at El-Hamet.

Colonel McLeod and the main force were stationed on the top of a hill, and detachment of fifty, thirty, and twenty men were posted round the base, in the strongest possible places, with orders to fall back on the main body if attacked. While so posted and before daylight, the enemy landed from their boats, surrounded the hill, and at once commenced the attack. Our men fought desperately, for they expected no quarter, and numbers fell. Captain Colin Mackay with his grenadier company commanded one of the outposts, and, like all the others, fought heroically; but his two subalterns, McCrae and Christie, and nearly half his men were soon killed. He himself received a fearful sabre cut in the neck (from which, although he lived for many years, he never completely recovered) and also a severe musket wound in the thigh, both of which rendered him at once prostrate. But Mackay's spirit was not gone, for he then ordered his few remaining men to leave him to die there, and to make the best of their retreat to the headquarters; but this they would not do, declaring to a man that they would sooner die with him, than leave him. Two of his remaining sergeants then got their captain on their shoulders and succeeded under a heavy fire in carrying him off in safety to the top of the hill, and there learnt that their Colonel was already amongst the slain.

The command then devolved upon a Major Vogalson (a German); he at once wished to surrender, fixing his white handkerchief on the top of his sword, as a sign of truce to the enemy. Colin Mackay lay under a gun bleeding and suffering severely from his wound, but he happily still retained his senses, and being told that Major Vogalson wished to surrender he cried out, "Soldiers, never, never while we have a round left!" upon which they cheered him again and again, and set Major Vogalson's authority completely aside; thus they actually continued to fight until the very last round of their ammunition was gone. The enemy pressed in upon them, and after a desperate struggle they were overpowered and obliged to surrender. The Turkish Pasha who commanded, then rode up and inquired, "Where is the brave man who has so long and so ably resisted me?" Colin Mackay, the hero of the day, was pointed out to him lying still in agony under a gun, on which Ali Pasha dismounted and, creeping near Mackay, took the sword off his own neck and shoulders and placed it gracefully on Mackay, saying, "You are indeed a brave man, and you deserve to wear my sword." From that time and long afterwards (although still a prisoner) he received the most marked attentions from the Pasha.

The few prisoners who survived were then secured, the dead were decapitated (and I fear many of the wounded also), and their living comrades were forced to carry their heads in sacks to the boats, and poor Colonel McLeod's conspicuous amongst the number. Most of the enemy then embarked with their prisoners and their trophies and returned in triumph to Cairo. There the heads of the dead were exhibited on poles for some weeks round the principal palaces of the authorities. The survivors were committed to confinement, and the officers were allowed at large on their paroles and treated well, especially Captain Mackay, who continued to receive the most marked attentions from every one. In this state they remained nearly eight months, when, after a variety of negotiations, they were exchanged and sent back to join us at Alexandria.

In another month the whole of our force left Egypt and returned to Sicily, far from proud of the result of our unfortunate and badly managed expedition. The 78th went to Messina, and, without landing, were ordered to Gibraltar, and on arrival there were sent direct to England.

Here I must mention that during the last eight months of our inactive life in Egypt our troops suffered much from ophthalmia. I was for many months laid up from that fearful malady, from which I suffer to this day, as I have partially lost the sight of my right eye; many of our men lost one, some both eyes, and became totally blind. From that period until now I have been subject to occasional attacks of inflammation of the eyes, so bad in 1821 and 1822 that I was recommended by my medical attendants to apply for a pension.

This I did through Lord Palmerston, then Secretary of War, on which I was ordered for treatment and report to Fort Pitt at Chatham, where for six weeks I was exposed to all kinds of pains and penalties. In consequence, I received a letter from Lord Palmerston saying that His Majesty was pleased to grant me the pension of an ensign, that being the rank I held when I received the injury to my sight. I wrote back to thank his lordship, but saying that, as the regulations for pensions had been changed, the amount now being allowed to increase with the rank of the individual so favoured, I still hoped, as I was now a captain, I should not be made a solitary exception to the rule. To this I received a reply ordering me again to Fort Pitt for treatment there. I remained under similar torture for another month. Soon after, I had a third reply, informing me that on the second report of the medical board His Majesty was pleased to grant me the pension of a lieutenant. I was then quartered in the Isle of Wight, so got leave of absence and went to London, determined in so good a cause to see Lord Palmerston in person. I was admitted, and then renewed my application and entreated his lordship to reconsider my case, adding that not only one eye was nearly gone but the other suffering much also.

He was writing at the time and never took his pen from his paper, yet he was very kind and appeared to listen to me attentively; then, looking up, said, "I must put you on half pay, sir, if you are so great a sufferer."

I said, "I hope not, my lord, while I am able to do my duty, as I have nothing else to depend upon but my commission."

He then smiled and said, "Well, write to me again, and I shall see what can be done." I did so, and in due course had the satisfaction to receive a notification stating that under the circumstances of my case His Majesty was graciously pleased to grant me the pension of a captain.

But to return from this long digression to where I left my early history in the brave 78th, I proceed to say that after finally leaving Gibraltar we arrived safely in Portsmouth and marched for Canterbury, a few months after to Chichester, and then to the Isle of Wight, where we detached in companies to all parts of the island. I was sent even further with a small detachment to Selsea barracks in Sussex, to take charge of a large ophthalmic depot of that station.

CHAPTER 5

The Battle of Talavera

I was not long at Selsea barracks before I wrote to the Horse Guards soliciting promotion, for I was then more than three years an ensign—an unusual period at that time. I received a sharp answer informing me that I ought to make my application through the officer commanding my regiment. This frightened me a little, for I now dreaded his displeasure also, for he was a perfect stranger to me. I had never seen him, having lately been appointed from another regiment. In a few days I regained confidence and made up my mind to write and tell my colonel frankly what I had done in ignorance of the rules of the service, and begging him to renew my application to the Horse Guards. I acted wisely, for a few weeks later I saw myself gazetted to a lieutenancy in the 24th Regiment, and being relieved of my command at Selsea, I joined that corps soon afterwards in Guernsey. This was in October, 1808; after remaining there till April, 1809, we embarked for Portugal to join the army under Sir Arthur Wellesley.

After a prosperous journey I found myself again in Lisbon. The march of the 24th to join the army was by a route along the banks of the Tagus, our principal halting-places being Villafranca, Azambuja, Cartaxo, Santarem, Abrantes, and Portalegre. We halted a month at Santarem, where we were most hospitably treated by the inhabitants. There, at a large convent, the mother abbess paid us great attention, and not only entertained us occasionally with fruits and sweetmeats, but allowed us daily to visit the convent and see the nuns. There was a large hall or reception-room, where visitors assembled, in which, at the far end, there was a large grated window in an unusually thick wall; both sides of the window were barred, but sufficiently open and lighted to enable us to see through the adjoining room. The nuns appeared in twos and threes in the inner room, and in this way we chatted and made love for hours daily, but the gratings between us were so far apart that we could only reach the tips of their fingers. It was during one of these visits that the mother abbess sent a privileged servant to lay out a table with fruit and cakes, and in return for all these favours we sent our band to play under the convent walls every other evening. We left Santarem with much regret.

We joined General John Ronald McKenzie's brigade, consisting (with the 24th) of the 31st and 45th Regiments; during the months of May and June we joined many other brigades and divisions of the army. Early in July the whole British force was concentrated and reviewed on the plains of Oropesa by the Spanish general, Cuesta, who proved afterwards a worthless man and a bad soldier, and yet he was then, by gross mismanagement and perhaps by the treachery of the Spanish Government, considered senior to Sir Arthur Wellesley. Our whole army in line at that review made a grand and magnificent appearance.

It was now known that the French army under General Marmont was not very far ahead of us, and every one believed we were now concentrated and advancing to the attack. These reports were soon confirmed by facts; after a few days of marching we found ourselves on the 23rd July encamped near the river Alberche, with General Cuesta's Spanish army on our right, the town and position of Talavera de la Reina a few miles in front on the opposite side of the river, with Marshal Marmont and the whole French army not far distant facing us.

It was afterwards well known that Sir Arthur Wellesley fully intended to cross the Alberche on the following morning and attack the enemy, but General Cuesta overruled any such advance on the pretence that the river was not fordable. It was then suspected that the real reason for delay was to allow the enemy time to fall back on his reinforcements.

On the 25th, when our advance was ordered and made, we found the water of the river only knee-deep; so we crossed, guns, cavalry, and infantry, without any difficulty, and heard that the French had actually retreated on reinforcements they expected from Madrid under King Joseph. Our main body was now halted, and in course of the day occupied the position of Talavera de la Reina; the whole of the Spanish army went on pretending to watch the movements of the enemy, while at the same time General Donkin's brigade and ours, consisting of the 87th and 88th Regiments, followed close upon the Spaniards with the intention of watching them!

We halted at Santa Olalla, eight or ten miles in front of Talavera, and there took up a strong position. The Spaniards continued their advance and marched farther. On the following noon we were astounded by seeing the whole Spanish army in confused mobs of hundreds retreating past us without any attempt at order or discipline, shouting that the French army was upon us. Our two brigades immediately got under arms and formed in line ready to receive the enemy, without making any attempt to stop the cowardly fugitives, and we soon lost sight of them. We remained firm in line till the French came well in sight; then we gave them a few volleys and retired in echelon of brigades, each halting occasionally and fronting as the ground favoured us, giving the enemy volley after volley.

This order of retreat was continued for some miles through a thickly wooded country. At last we got upon a most extensive plain, keeping the same order till the enemy affronted and opened a heavy fire, but fortunately their guns fell short, and we returned the fire with more success, and soon we saw our own gallant army drawn up in order on the heights and grounds near Talavera. This cheered us, and we continued our retreat and defence in the most perfect order. It was a most splendid sight; on nearing the main position of our army a considerable body of our cavalry advanced to meet us, and our batteries from the heights opened a heavy and destructive fire at the enemy.

Then commenced in earnest the glorious battle of Talavera, on the 27th July, 1809. The enemy made several deployments of their numerous columns during the action, attacking with desperation almost every part of our extended line, but on every occasion they failed and were driven back; yet fresh troops were brought up, the battle raged furiously, and there was much slaughter on both sides. I was slightly wounded in the thigh just as we got into our own lines.

On the morning of the 28th a heavy and constant cannonade was commenced, and the battle was renewed with more vigour. The French columns came on boldly and tried again and again to walk over us and break our lines, but we defied them, and at every assault they were driven back with fearful slaughter; then they advanced with fresh troops, cheering and shouting "*Vive l'Empereur!*" The others, disheartened by our determined resistance, faced about with the altered cry "*Sauve qui peut.*" The slaughter on both sides was fearful butchering work, and was continued by both armies the whole of that memorable day. Our loss in men was unusually great, and the French loss was said to be greater than ours. When the morning of the 29th dawned, not a Frenchman was to be seen! Their whole army had retired during the night of the 28th! leaving us the victors and masters of the field of battle.

A fearful and most distressing sight that field presented as we went over it, covered with thousands of the enemy's dead as well as our own, and thousands of wounded, numbers with their clothes entirely or partially burnt off their bodies from the dry grass on which they lay having caught fire from the bursting of shells during the action; there were many of the wounded who could not crawl away and escape. Those who still lived were at once removed, and the dead were buried. We remained on the field of battle three days more, attending to the wounded. Having then received information that Marshal Soult with the French army was at Plasencia and advancing on us, our whole army was put in retreat towards Portugal by Truxhillo, Arzobispo, and Merida, leaving the wounded and many medical officers in hospitals at Talavera. The road taken was across country, and so bad that we were obliged to employ pioneers and strong working parties to enable us to get on. From these unavoidable causes and delays, our marches on many days did not exceed ten miles, and our provisions became very limited. We had much rain, and our men suffered much from sickness, fevers, agues, and dysentery; the latter was much increased by the quantity of raw Indian corn and wild honey which the country produced, and which the soldiers consumed in spite of every threat and order to the contrary.

This retreat lasted three weeks, and I never remember seeing more general suffering and sickness. On crossing the bridge of Arzobispo we met a division of the Spanish army driving before them a herd of many hundreds of swine. Our men broke loose from their ranks as if by instinct, surrounded the pigs, and in defiance of all orders and authority, the men seized each a pig, and cut it up immediately into several pieces; so each secured their mess for that day, then again fell into place in the ranks, as if nothing had happened—this in open defiance of the continued exertions and threats of all their officers, from the general downwards. The Spaniards stood still in amazement, evidently in doubt whether they should attempt to avenge their losses, but they did not do so, and each army continued its march in opposite directions. When we camped for the night our good soldiers sent a liberal portion of their spoil to each of their officers, nor were the generals forgotten! and they, like the youngest of us, were thankful, at that time, for so good a mess. We continued our retreat by Elvas and Badajoz, then halted at various stages, and were quartered in the different towns and villages on the banks of the Guadiana for some months afterwards.

Chapter 6

The Battle of Busaco

We were now in Portugal, and by the kindness and hospitality of the inhabitants were made truly comfortable. We felt this change, for in Spain we were always received coolly, and got nothing in the way of food from the inhabitants upon whom we were quartered, whereas in Portugal we were received and welcomed with open arms by every one; whether rich or poor, these good people upon whom we were billeted always shared their food with us, and gave us freely of the best of every sort of provisions they had.

Towards the end of this year (1809) the army was again in motion for the north of Portugal, and after a variety of marches and changes of quarters my division halted at Vizeu, Mangualde, Anseda, Linhares, and Celorico; at each of these places we had abundance of provisions and supplies and were, by the kindness of the inhabitants, most comfortable. Some time before this, the 31st and 45th Regiments were removed from our brigade and replaced by the 42nd and 61st Regiments.

Our troops remained inactive till about the beginning of July, 1810; then we heard that the French army, greatly reinforced, was advancing upon us under Marshal Massena. They were checked for a time by some hard fighting with our advance light division, under General Crawford, also by continued resistance of the garrisons of Ciudad Rodrigo and Almeida. The former was occupied generally by Spanish troops and some Portuguese militia, the latter fortress by one English regiment and three or four Portuguese regiments, with brave Colonel Cox, of our service, as the governor. Both these forts resisted gallantly and successfully for a short time, but after a siege of a fortnight Ciudad Rodrigo surrendered, and in ten days more the principal magazines and public buildings in Almeida were levelled to the ground by a sudden explosion, killing five hundred troops and inhabitants and destroying the principal works and means of defence; in this state of confusion and terror the brave governor, Colonel Cox, was obliged to capitulate. It was afterwards discovered that this shame and sacrifice was occasioned by the treachery of one of the Portuguese officers, who was actually the lieutenant-governor of the fort, and who openly headed a mutiny of the garrison against the governor, Colonel Cox, aided and assisted by another Portuguese officer, who was the chief of the artillery, and who had been for some time in secret correspondence with France!

The surrender of these two important strongholds encouraged the enemy to renew their advance, so that in the beginning of September Lord Wellington commenced his able and well-devised retreat on the Lines of Torres Vedras, within thirty miles of Lisbon. The Portuguese army under General Beresford and the Spaniards under the Marquis de la Romana, retreating on our flank for the same destination, all believed that we were making the best of our way to our ships for embarkation, and with the full intention of finally quitting the country. So secretly had the works of the Lines of Torres Vedras been carried on, that only rumours of their existence were heard, and those only by very few officers of high rank. It was even said that neither the English nor Portuguese Government knew anything positive about these works nor where they were constructed, and I remember well that most of our officers laughed at the idea of our remaining in Portugal, and heavy bets were daily made, during our retreat, on the chances or the certainty of our embarkation. But different indeed were the results, and all the world soon acknowledged the master-mind of our most noble and gallant commander.

I have said that we commenced this retreat early in September, disputing the ground daily as opportunities offered, and as we were covered by our Light Division, these brave men had nearly all the hard work and most of the fighting, but, when necessary, other troops were brought up to their support, and occasionally to relieve them from this constant harassing duty. For a few days the Portuguese militia under Colonel Trant and the Spaniards under the Marquis de la Romana were constantly kept to guard our flanks. In this way the main body, by different roads, retreated in good order for twenty or thirty miles a day, most of the inhabitants leaving their homes and property and falling back in thousands before us, rich and poor, men, women, and children, carrying little with them beyond the clothing on their backs, and halting and bivouacking in the open fields, a short distance before us, whenever the army halted for the night.

A month after we started, our division was suddenly moved off the main line of road, from the crossing of the Mondego River above Coimbra, to the mountain position of the Sierra de Busaco, some miles farther in rear of the above river and city; all the other divisions of the army were directed to the same point.

Having scrambled up that mountain as best we could, our whole army was soon formed in order of battle. Below us was an extensive open but thickly wooded country, and there we saw the whole of the French army, under General Massena, advancing in many columns to attack us. The Sierra de Busaco is a very extensive range of mountains, and the main road from Coimbra, passes over the centres of it, to the interior; but in all the other places it is so precipitous and rocky, that our gallant old commander was obliged to be carried up in a blanket by four sergeants, for no horse could ascend there.

By two o'clock on the afternoon of the 27th September our whole army was in position, our guns in battery, and our light troops thrown out in front for some distance. These arrangements were not long completed when the French, in different columns, advanced to attack, covered by clouds of their light troops and skirmishers. As soon as they came within range they commenced the battle with continued rounds from their numerous artillery, and our batteries returned the compliment. The skirmishers of both armies opened their fire furiously, and two of their columns pushed forward up the most easy and accessible part of the mountain with drums playing and endless cheers, and appeared as if determined to carry all before them.

Our lines stood firm and retained their fire till the enemy came within easy range; they then gave a general volley, followed by a thundering, well-directed independent file firing, covered by our artillery, which soon made the enemy halt, stagger, and hesitate, and in a few minutes they were seen to face about and to retire in very good order. Their loss must have been great, and so was ours.

At daylight on the morning of the 28th the battle was again renewed in a more extended and general way by the enemy, for they attacked simultaneously several points of our position; at the same time column after column was seen pressing up the mountain in every direction, and in one place so successfully, that at break of day one of the heaviest and largest of these actually managed to reach within a few yards of our position before it was seen by our troops. They were no sooner seen than received with a volley; yet they gallantly kept their ground, and returned our fire without ceasing for about half an hour; during that time neither of the contending lines advanced, nor gave way one inch. At last our men were ordered to charge; then the enemy retired, and, at the point of the bayonet, were driven down the hill pell-mell, in the greatest confusion, leaving many hundreds of their dead and wounded behind them. Their other minor columns of attack were repulsed in like manner. In course of that day the battle was again renewed, and the French were finally driven back, although they fought ably and with much gallantry.

During this day's battle our invincible and gallant Commander-in-Chief, Lord Wellington, pulled up with all his staff in front of my regiment, and dismounted, directing one of his orderlies to do the same and to hold his horse steady by the bridle. He then placed his field-glass in rest over his saddle, and for some minutes continued coolly and quietly to reconnoitre the enemy, and this under a heavy fire!

On the morning of the 29th there was not a Frenchman to be seen. They had retired during the night, and were soon known to be moving to turn the left of our position, so as to cut off our retreat by Coimbra and the main road. But our "master-mind and head" was equal to the occasion, and in another hour the whole of our army was in retreat by a different route, to cross the Mondego River at and above Coimbra. This we did many hours before the enemy could reach us.

For days we kept possession of Coimbra and the neighbouring banks of the Mondego, to give our faithful friends the inhabitants time to destroy, bury, or remove their valuables, and above all their provisions, lest they should fall into the hands of the enemy. These arrangements were made from the commencement of our retreat, and strictly carried out by the inhabitants. They left their homes and accompanied the army, taking with them only a few of their valuables. Before reaching Torres Vedras I remember seeing many of these noble patriots, rich and poor, all barefooted and in rags. When we finally halted they went to Lisbon.

These arrangements were more distressing to General Massena than all the fighting and opposition he met with, for he was so sure of driving us into the sea, or forcing us to embark, that he left his principal magazines of provisions behind, confident of finding sufficient supplies in the country through which he passed. In all these hopes and speculations he was indeed sadly disappointed; the consequence was that they were sorely tried, and suffered much from their limited and always uncertain commissariat.

We arrived at the Lines of Torres Vedras on the 10th and 11th of October, closely pursued by the enemy, their advance guards and our rear troops constantly skirmishing, and causing some loss to them and to us; but we always found time to bury our dead and carry away the wounded.

We had no sooner taken up our relative positions than we were surprised and amazed at the formidable and strong appearance of the temporary works in which we found ourselves, and which we soon learnt extended in a direct line for thirty miles from Alhandra, on the banks of the Tagus, to Mafra, on the sea coast, thus covering Lisbon completely, from the broad and deep river on one side to the wide ocean on the other, this line forming in most places a continuous chain of rising ground. My division (the 1st) was stationed at headquarters, Sobral, about the centre of the lines. By this happy chance we had an opportunity of seeing Lord Wellington daily, and of sharing his dinners occasionally, in our turn, for he made a point of asking the juniors as well as the senior officers; and dinner then, with good wine, was worth having! Yet upon the whole we fared very well, for we had a good and regular supply from Lisbon.

CHAPTER 7

The Lines of Torres Vedras

The French were up and in position along our whole line. The next day Marshal Massena massed the strongest of his columns in front of our most formidable works, and desperate attacks were made on various parts of our line, but these, after hours of hard fighting, were always repulsed. The rest of each day was spent in staring at each other and watching the movements of the enemy, and frequently by a heavy cannonade for hours by both armies. Our loss was considerable; and from the French deserters, who were very numerous at this time, we learnt that their killed and wounded far exceeded ours, and that they were suffering much from sickness and want of provisions. In this way we remained constantly on the defensive, and frequently fighting, for upwards of four months, our army keeping our own ground and never attempting to attack the enemy, and always driving them back with much slaughter whenever they advanced to storm or carry away any of our works. During these operations the Marquis de la Romana, with his division of the Spanish army, joined us.

When we had been so employed for about two months, an authority reached Lord Wellington from England to confer the honour of knighthood on General Beresford, then the Commander-in-Chief of the Portuguese army. A general order was issued by Lord Wellington inviting one-third of the combined armies of England, Spain, and Portugal to assemble at the royal palace of Mafra, on a given day, to witness the ceremony of General Beresford being knighted, which stated that the Commander-in-Chief intended to return to his post at an early hour that night, and wished every officer to do the same, and concluded with an expression of his confidence that the remaining generals and officers of the army who were left at their posts would do their duty if attacked by the enemy during his absence.

I was one of the happy ones who took advantage of this invitation, and at an early hour on the day named I started for the palace of Mafra, a distance of about fifteen miles. On our arrival there we found not only many hundreds of officers—English, Spanish, and Portuguese—but also a great portion of the Portuguese nobility, all come to do honour to the occasion, Lord Wellington and his brilliant staff amongst them; and, what was more remarkable, large masses of the French army not a quarter of a mile away from us, with their advanced piquets and sentries, were looking quietly and coolly on at our gathering, and although our visitors from Lisbon advanced in crowds as near as possible to look and stare at them in turn, not the slightest attempt was made by our brave enemies to alarm or disturb them. The same consideration and courtesy was continued during the whole of that memorable occasion, so I think to this day that the good feeling and understanding must have been previously arranged between Lord Wellington and General Massena.

As soon as the whole company had arrived, as many as could be got in were assembled in the principal hall of the palace; then appeared Lord Wellington with General Beresford on his arm, followed by a numerous suite of general officers and Portuguese nobility, and the Commander-in-Chief's personal staff. A circle was formed in the centre of the hall, into which all the grandees entered. His Majesty's commands were then read, on which General Beresford knelt down, and Lord Wellington, drawing his sword, waved it over the General's head, saying, "Arise, Sir William Carr Beresford," and ended so far the imposing pageant. Then was opened a folding door, displaying many tables laid out with a most recherché dinner and choice wines for at least five hundred people. I was one of the fortunate ones who succeeded in getting early admission. Then dancing was commenced, and kept on without ceasing until daylight. Our popular commander danced without ever resting, and appeared thoroughly to enjoy himself, though he retired at midnight, and many followed his example; but by far the greater number remained till morning, much to the delight of all the lovely and illustrious donnas and senoras of Lisbon. The night was very dark, and many officers going home lost their way and got into the enemy's lines, but on stating whence they came, were all treated most kindly, and at daylight were allowed with hearty good wishes to proceed to their respective quarters.

For many weeks after this we continued in the Lines of Torres Vedras receiving the enemy's attacks, and after many hard struggles invariably driving them back in confusion. At last Marshal Massena saw he could neither force our position, nor hope for any lasting success by continuing his efforts, so about the middle of January, 1811, being known to be sorely tried for supplies and provisions, he retreated with his army thirty miles or more, then established his headquarters at Santarem, the approach to which he at once fortified.

We followed without delay and fixed our headquarters at Cartaxo, within ten miles of Santarem, with one Light Division in front and in sight of the enemy. The remaining corps were distributed on the various roads to our right and left, following and watching the movements of our foes; and so we continued for two months, without anything important being done. Our Light Division did make some attempt to force the enemy's advance position in front of Santarem. This was a narrow causeway nearly a quarter of a mile long, built with stone and lime over the centre of an extensive bog or morass, very soft and knee-deep in water, at the enemy's end being strongly fortified with numerous covering breastworks and guns in battery; but each attack failed with considerable loss to us.

For some weeks no further efforts were made in this direction, for after a long reconnaissance it was believed that the storming and carrying of such a place would entail a fearful sacrifice of life. It was then determined to make one more effort, and the three grenadier companies of my brigade were told off to lead the advance of the storming party across the causeway.

For this perilous duty we marched off one morning before daylight to a certain rendezvous in a wood near the site of our intended operations. There we found, in considerable numbers, masses of infantry and many guns in battery, ready to support us, and a part of the Light Division prepared to flank our advance, by taking at once the swamps and marshes, and so clearing the way for other troops to follow with the hope of turning both the enemy's flanks and getting into their rear, while we, the storming party, at the double, with our powerful supports, should pass the causeway and storm and carry the enemy's stronghold and batteries at the end of it.

All was well arranged, and willing and ready were all to make the attempt; but fortunately for many of us, just about the appointed hour for our advance it came on to rain heavily, and so continued without ceasing for some hours after daylight. As we could no longer conceal our movements from the enemy, this attack was given up, and we marched back to our quarters without any loss, but with a good wetting. Had the attack taken place our loss would have been terribly heavy.

The most happy feeling prevailed between our Light Division and the French advanced posts and garrison at Santarem. Many of our officers used to go by special invitation to pass their evenings at the theatre with the French officers at Santarem, and on every such occasion were treated in the most hospitable manner, and always returned well pleased with their visits. Of course, the sanction of the Commanders-in-Chief of both armies was given to this intimacy. The Marquis de la Romana died at Cartaxo while we were there, and was laid in state for many days, and buried with much splendour and all military honours.

While here our "patrone," the owner of our house, used to visit us very frequently. One morning, while he was present, I was sitting before the fire and poking with the tongs at the back of the chimney, when suddenly it gave way, exposing a tin box, on which "*patrone*" called out in alarm, "*Mio dinhero! mio dinhero!*" and at once seized it; but we insisted on seeing the contents, and found a considerable sum of money, the poor man's all, and of course we restored it to him. When the French were advancing some months before, most of the inhabitants hid their treasures much in the same way.

I was one morning taking an early walk with Lieutenant Hunt, of my regiment, in the immediate neighbourhood of Cartaxo, when we observed in a field a mule and a donkey grazing; not far off was a Portuguese peasant. I called him and asked to whom the animals belonged; he said he did not know, but that he believed they had strayed from the French lines, so I told him to drive them up to my quarters, and that I would give him a few dollars for his trouble.

Chapter 8

The Lost Regimental Books

I must now tell a more creditable story. At this time I commanded a company, and had also unofficially the charge of the accounts and payments of another company, the captain having a great dislike to bookkeeping.

In those days the military chest of the army was so low that the troops were frequently two or three months in arrear of pay; but the soldiers' accounts were regularly made up and balanced every month, and carried forward ready for payment when money was available. I was then sufficiently lucky to have a donkey of my own, although before this I was, like most subalterns, contented to share a donkey or mule with another officer, for the carriage of our limited baggage and spare provision; the Government allowing us forage for one animal between every two subalterns, and one ration of forage to each captain. My good and trusty beast carried two hampers covered with tarpaulin, on which was printed most distinctly my name, "Lieutenant Anderson, 24th Regiment," and in these I carried not only my few changes of clothes and spare provisions, but also my two companies' books, ledgers, etc., and at that time about two hundred dollars in cash.

We had all native servants at this time; mine, a Portuguese boy, was always in charge of my baggage and donkey. The day we marched into Cartaxo, all the baggage arrived in due course except mine, and for some hours we could hear nothing of my boy nor of my donkey. At last, about dusk, he came up crying, and told me he had lost my all.

I waited for many days, still hoping to hear something of my property, but all to no purpose. There were no records kept of the soldiers' accounts except the company's ledgers, so I was thus, in consequence of my loss, entirely at the mercy of my men, and had no other course left to me but to parade my own, and then the other company, and explain the situation, and my confidence in them all, and then to take from their own lips the amount of balances, debit or credit, of their respective accounts. I committed their statements at once to paper, but of course I could not say if they were correct or not. I then gave up all hope of ever seeing my lost property again.

I was advised to request the adjutant-general of the army to circulate a memorandum in General Orders, describing my donkey and baggage, and offering a handsome reward for discovery, recovery, or for any information respecting them.

A few days afterwards I received a letter from a corporal of the 5th Dragoon Guards, stationed at Azambuja, informing me that on the very evening of my loss he found my donkey feeding in a cornfield near his quarters; soon afterwards, seeing two soldiers of the 24th Regiment, he asked them if they knew Lieutenant Anderson; being told that they did, he asked if they would take charge of the donkey, to which they willingly consented, so he gave all over to them, with directions to be sure to deliver them in safety.

This letter I at once took to my commanding officer, who ordered me to go without delay to Azambuja to see the corporal, and ask if he thought he could remember and identify the men.

I rode off alone through a wild country, a distance of twenty miles, got to Azambuja in good time that evening, and found the corporal, whose name I cannot now remember. He expressed great surprise at my not having received the things, as more than a month had passed since he had given them over to the two men of the 24th. He said one was a grenadier and the other a battalion man, that he had not noticed them much, but thought he might be able to point them out.

On this I went to General Sir Lowry Cole and told him my story; he at once ordered the corporal to accompany me back to Cartaxo. That evening we started under heavy rain, and rode all night. The corporal was a tall and powerful man, and I must confess that I felt a little afraid of him. The night was very dark, and the ride for many miles was through a long wood. I more than once thought that if the corporal was himself the thief he might now dispose of me without any one being the wiser, so I ordered him to ride some distance in front, on pretence of looking for the road, so as to give me time for a bolt should he turn upon me. My fears proved ungenerous and unfounded, for without any accident we arrived at Cartaxo.

I reported myself to my commanding officer, who ordered the adjutant to parade the whole regiment in front of my quarters. This was done, and man after man was called in for the corporal's inspection, then passed out by a back door, without any communication with those still outside. After about a hundred had passed, the corporal, looking at the next man who entered, said, "I'll swear this is one of them." The accused became at once indignant and insolent, denying all knowledge of the charge. He was searched, and a few dollars were found between his coat and the lining, but these he said he got, like most soldiers, in course of the war.

The adjutant then proceeded to call in the remaining men; at last the corporal fixed his eyes on one of the men who entered, and said, "This is the other man; I feel sure these are the two men; I'll swear to them both."

This was a private of the grenadiers, and he, like the other, boldly denied the charge. Both were then secured and sent under escort to the guard-house, and were given till twelve o'clock to make a full confession; if they did not, they would be brought to a general court-martial, and would be shot if found guilty. They both knew that such tragic ends were then by no means uncommon. They were also told the serious inconvenience and loss which their officers and fellow-soldiers had sustained, and if they would tell how the books could be recovered the commanding officer would be as easy as possible with them, and that Mr. Anderson did not care much for the rest of the things. But still they denied, swearing vengeance on the corporal. At last they saw their danger and sent for the sergeant-major and made a full confession, saying they knew there was money in the hampers, and that tempted them; they had led the donkey into a wood near Azambuja, tied him to a tree, taken the money, and buried the hampers and all their contents on the spot, and offered to show the place.

I was ordered to march the two prisoners under a strong escort to the wood they mentioned, and there we found, still tied to the tree, the skeleton of my poor donkey, dead for at least a month. We began to dig, and soon came upon my long-lost and precious hampers, and found everything destroyed by the rain, but the books, though greatly injured, were still legible.

We marched back to Cartaxo, and on arrival the prisoners were recommitted to the guard-house. My next care was to compare the verbal statements given to me by the men with the original accounts in the ledgers; and here comes the cream of my long story, and my reasons for going into this lengthy digression. To their honour, therefore, be it told, there was not half-a-crown's difference between the accounts in the ledgers and those given by each soldier from memory, the voluntary statements of no less than a hundred and fifty men! I consider this a great proof of the general honesty and integrity of the British soldier. The two prisoners were brought before a regimental court-martial, found guilty, and sentenced to corporal punishment and to be put under stoppages of pay until the money taken from me was made good. The former they suffered, but I never got back a shilling of my money. One of them died some months afterwards from wounds received at the battle of Fuentes d'Onoro, and the other was killed by another soldier in a boxing match.

We remained at Cartaxo, with the armies in the various relative positions which I have already described, and without any great fighting, until the morning of the 7th March, 1811, when we heard that the main body of the French army had been for some days retreating, and that their headquarters, under Marshal Massena, and their rearguard had that morning retired from Santarem.

Chapter 9

The Battle of Fuentes D'Onoro

The whole of our troops were put en route to follow them. The 1st Light Division and our headquarters and brilliant staff were all much excited, and anxious to be at them. We soon arrived at, and crossed without opposition, the formidable causeway and works which so long defied us, and which even now startled us not a little. In a few hours more we were passing through the now empty and deserted town of Santarem. We were now halted, and could not see much, but amongst the many signs of devastation and plunder we passed under the remaining walls of that once peaceful convent where, two years ago, we had spent many happy days and hours. Nothing now remained but the bare crumbling walls. The dear nuns were gone, no one knew where, most likely to Lisbon. The building was destroyed and plundered by the enemy, and we afterwards heard that such was the fate of all the convents within reach of the French during their advance towards the Lines of Torres Vedras, and that many of the nuns who had not time to escape, or who trusted to their religion and calling for protection and safety, were shamefully treated by the French officers and soldiers. Of this I can have little doubt, for when our advance was over, and we got settled amongst the inhabitants, we heard many sad stories of this description.

We had not advanced many miles from Santarem when we heard the distant firing of our Light Division and our advanced field train, now evidently up with the enemy. This went on till dusk, and we then bivouacked for the night. Next morning we were again in pursuit, without pressing the enemy, rather to allow them to get away, unless they offered battle. Their first stand was for some hours in force in front of the village of Pombal. As soon as our troops got within reach they opened a heavy fire from a numerous artillery upon us, but our troops and guns, being now well up, returned the compliment with their accustomed vigour and interest; some manoeuvring and changes of position followed on the part of the French, and additional troops were shown and brought into action. Our 1st Division was then hurried to the front to support our troops, and having got into action, the fight was continued with determined valour for some time, until the enemy began to give way, and finally to retreat in some confusion. We followed them till dusk, when we halted and took up our position for the night. For days after this we had no fighting, till we drove them across the Mondego at Coimbra, and by some other bridges and fords of that splendid river, at each of which places there was a great deal of fighting.

The scenes of destruction and murder which we frequently passed in the villages and on our daily march, were dreadful. Houses and furniture burnt, men and women mutilated and murdered, lying about in the most disgusting and barbarous manner, some with their throats cut, some with their eyes and ears gone, and others cut up and most dreadfully exposed; all this for revenge, because they would not, or could not, supply the French army with provisions, and in the hope that these savage proceedings would terrify others into instant compliance.

The French were suffering fearfully at that time from want of food, and their deserters to us were then unusually numerous. We had almost daily evidence of the former fact, for as we entered villages which they had left, it was an ordinary sight to see in the houses one or more dead French soldiers lying on the floor in full uniform, their arms still grasped in their hands as if asleep, also sitting in chairs with their caps on, and in full uniform, their firelocks standing upright between their legs, and quite dead; evidently they had died from want of food.

I may mention that during our pursuit of the enemy we always took up our position each night in the open fields, without any covering beyond our blankets, and these were generally saturated with wet, for in Portugal rains are frequent, and dews and fogs unusually heavy during the night. If we remained for a few days or weeks we cut down some trees and bushes and made ourselves as comfortable as we could in shelters. In permanent quarters the army was always housed in the neighbouring towns and villages. When the towns and villages were deserted we were distributed among a number of empty houses and streets.

The country abounded with game, especially hares, so during our idle time we were coursing or shooting with success. Each company cooked its own food, and divided it in the usual form. The officers of one or two companies messed together, giving and taking dinner with their friends occasionally.

We arrived near the frontiers of Portugal driving the enemy before us, passing through Vizeu, Mangualde, Celorico, and Guarda, and some of the other villages we had occupied. The army was halted for some weeks, and many of the inhabitants joined us and again occupied their houses, but in all of these places we found the same sad evidence of the reckless destruction of houses and property of every description.

When we reached the town of Sabugal on the Coa we found the enemy strongly posted to dispute our passage of that river. After a good deal of fighting our Light Division forced and carried the bridge, and a general engagement for some hours followed, with much slaughter on both sides. In the evening the enemy gave way and continued the retreat. It rained fearfully during the night. In the fields which my brigade occupied we were up to our ankles in mud. It was one of the most trying nights we ever had; our men suffered so much from the wet and cold that two or three were found dead on the ground when the assembly sounded next morning. Massena halted his army again in the neighbourhood of Ciudad Rodrigo and Almeida, in both of which fortresses he had a strong garrison; there he was allowed to remain unmolested for some months longer. We in like manner halted, and were put in quarters in the different villages in advance of the Coa, my brigade being comfortably housed at Alfaiates, and while here we enjoyed ourselves much in field sports and coursing.

Headquarters were again near us, and Lord Wellington mixed frequently with us in the chase. Our quartermaster got sick about this time, and I was appointed to do his duty, which gave me an opportunity of improving my Portuguese.

About the last week in April, 1811, the army was again put in motion to the front. Early on the morning of the 3rd of May we came in sight of the French army posted in order of battle in and beyond the village of Fuentes d'Onoro. The weather was beautiful, and both armies fought without either gaining any decided advantage. On that day the casualties on both sides were numerous, when night stopped the battle. Next morning at daylight it was renewed, and continued at various intervals in various parts of the line, until again checked by darkness. On the following morning, the 5th of May, it began again in earnest, and was more formidable and general, the numbers of killed and wounded and prisoners on both sides being very considerable. Upon the whole the French gained ground upon us, where my brigade and divisions were posted, and drove us from the village of Fuentes. This occurred about midday, and the weather being unusually hot, a suspension of hostilities was agreed upon for the purpose of carrying away the wounded and burying the dead.

I had charge of one of the fatigue parties sent on this service, and passed at once over to the village of Fuentes, then in possession of the enemy, from which they had driven us. We were received most kindly, and proceeded at once to our work of burying the dead and removing the wounded. This was continued for only an hour, when the bugles of both armies sounded "To arms!" on which the French troops near us immediately fell in, shouldered their arms, and taking off their caps, gave us three cheers. We at the same time, shaking hands with some of them, made off as fast as we could back to our own lines, and there, forming in order of battle, took off our caps and returned the same hearty good cheers. Then, and not until then, was a shot fired by either of the contending parties, and the battle again commenced with more vigour than ever, and continued with fearful slaughter until night.

Amongst our losses on that memorable day was a very dear friend of mine, Lieutenant Edmond Kelly Ireland, of the 24th Regiment. I was with him when he fell, and I knew where to find him. He was equally well loved and regretted by all his brother officers, and Lieutenants Moorsoom and Pell and I, after a talk, determined to go at once to the French lines to claim his body; so, accompanied by two of our soldiers carrying a blanket, and without leave, we moved boldly off to the French side until stopped by one of their sentries. We answered "English officers," on which he ordered us to stand still, then turned out his guard, or picquet. A French officer and a dozen men then advanced, and asked who we were and what we wanted, and being told we came to request to be allowed to look for and claim the body of an officer and friend of ours who fell that day on their ground, our brave foe said at once, "Certainly, gentlemen; give me up your swords and I shall be happy to conduct you wherever you wish to go."

We accompanied him under escort to his bush hut. He spoke freely and kindly of the battle, boasting a little that they had driven us off so much of the ground and from the village. He gave us a glass of brandy and water and biscuits, then said, "Gentlemen, I shall now conduct you where you like," so off we went to the spot where I knew poor Ireland fell. We soon recognized him amongst heaps of slain; he was lying on his back stripped of all his clothing.

He was shot right through the head, and must have died at once. We placed him in the blanket and carried him back with us, returning as we came, by the French officers' bivouac, there receiving our swords. In a quarter of an hour more we were safely back in our own lines, without having been missed. Our next work was to dig a grave, and that being damp and watery, we opened another in a higher ground, and there we laid our dear and much lamented friend. Our doings soon became known; some one told all to our colonel, who at once assembled all the officers, and gave us a most severe lecture, pointing out to us how improper and imprudent our conduct was, and how difficult it would have been, if we had fallen into the hands of a dishonourable enemy, to prove that we were not deserters, and we were cautioned not to attempt any such folly for the future. Later, we were told by one of the senior officers that, although obliged to reprimand us, no one thought more highly of our conduct than our good Colonel Kelly. We fully expected to renew the fight on the morning of the 6th, but to our surprise and satisfaction, as that day dawned not a Frenchman was to be seen. They retired beyond our reach during the night, and so ended the battle of Fuentes d'Onoro, fought on the 3rd, 4th, and 5th of May, 1811.

Chapter 10

In Scotland

We remained a week or more in the neighbourhood. The whole army was then again put in motion towards the south-east of Portugal, in consequence of the state of affairs previous to the battle of Albuera, under Marshal Beresford. The weather during a part of this march was very wet and stormy; our army suffered much from fever and ague. I was myself amongst the number, and was attacked so severely that after some days' suffering, without any covering or shelter, I was ordered to the rear and then on sick leave, in December, 1811, and I arrived in Plymouth in January, 1812.

My leave was for six months, which enabled me to visit my father and friends in Scotland. I was ordered to join the depot of my regiment at Maldon, in Essex, and soon after I was sent with a recruiting party to Dornoch, in my own native country. Lieut.-General Sir David Baird was then the colonel-in-chief of my regiment, and he thought that by sending me with a party to the Highlands I might find some countrymen for his regiment; but in this both he and I were disappointed, for I remained at Dornoch four months and never got a man. I was now ordered to leave my recruiting party with an officer of the 21st Regiment and to proceed to the Isle of Wight to embark for India to join the first battalion of my regiment. This most unexpected official letter reached me while actually at a public ball;

but I determined to enjoy myself for at least one night, so danced away till six in the morning, then went to bed and slept till nine, when I started on foot on a journey of seventy miles (two-thirds of which was over Highland moors and mountains) without even a path to guide me; but I was then young, and, moreover, I fancied myself in love, and that gave me heart and vigour to push on. In the last forty miles I was obliged to have a guide, and having walked the whole of that day and night, I completed my journey in twenty-four hours. I may also mention that my lady-love was at this time the acknowledged belle of all the country, but for various reasons our courtship ended in nothing beyond a sincere and friendly feeling, even to this day. I found another official letter countermanding my orders for India and directing me to return with my recruiting party and rejoin the depot at Maldon. Six weeks after this the remains of my regiment returned from Portugal and were quartered at Chelmsford, in Essex, and there we joined soon after.

General W. P. Acland commanded the district, and soon ordered an inspection of the regiment. When he came to the companies' books he was so much displeased with the irregular and imperfect manner in which they were kept that he found fault with all except Lieutenant Anderson's books, and ordered all the officers to be confined to barracks until our lieutenant-colonel could report that the books were properly posted and ready for his final inspection. This was a great triumph for me, and much good, as I shall presently show, came out of it; for in about a month England was sending a considerable force to Holland, and amongst the staff for that service General Acland's brigade-major was included. On the following day I was actually marching off in charge of our barrack guard, when an orderly arrived to say the general wished to see me at once. Another unfortunate officer was then crossing the barrack yard with his gun on his shoulder, going with others on a shooting excursion, but as he was next for duty he was ordered to get ready at once to take my place in charge of the guard, much to his annoyance.

I repaired at once to the general's quarters, and on being shown in he said, "My brigade-major has been ordered away, and I want you to come and assist me at the brigade office until a successor is appointed." I thanked him, and said I should be most happy to attend and do my best.

He then took me to the office and made me copy some returns; in course of the day he looked in, examined my work, and ordered me to come to him every morning. Here I must mention that beyond dining with him occasionally in my turn with the other officers of the garrison, I knew nothing of General Acland, nor he of me; but now, being nominally on his staff, I used to ride with him and dine with him more frequently, and so began to feel myself a great man, for I had much to do, having no less than six regiments and depots in the district, the reports and correspondence all passing through my hands; and my responsibilities and duties were increased by the general's frequent absence in London and other places, on which occasions he always authorized me to act in his name and to carry on all correspondence and duties as if he were present, except that if any unusual thing occurred, or any official letter arrived requiring his opinion and decision, I was to forward all such matters to his address, which he always left with me. I was also to keep his absence a secret from every one. In this way I got on most happily, when one morning he asked me, "How long have you been in this service, and what service have you seen?" I told him, and that my first battle was under him, as commanding my brigade at Maida. This seemed to surprise him, for he was not aware of my having been at Maida.

He then said, "Bring me a memorandum in writing of your services." I did so on the following morning, without suspecting what use he was going to make of it. Conceive, then, my joy and surprise in seeing myself a fortnight afterwards gazetted as captain of a company in the York Chasseurs. Of course, I thanked my benefactor with all my heart and soul; but he only said, with his accustomed kindness, "You deserve it, and I hope you will get on." This was not all, for he next applied to the Horse Guards to have me permanently confirmed as his brigade-major; but that was refused on the ground that I was appointed to a new regiment where experienced officers were immediately required, and therefore I must join at Sandown barracks in the Isle of Wight with as little delay as possible. Still, he kept me for some weeks longer with him. At last the time came when I was obliged to leave. He then asked me to write to him occasionally, but he lived only for three years after. I did write repeatedly, and as often heard from him, and it is in fond and grateful acknowledgment of my much-lamented friend that I gave my dear son the name of Acland. Had I never seen General Acland I would not have been a captain for ten years or more.

On joining the York Chasseurs at Sandown barracks I was pleased at finding the officers a fine set of young fellows, all promoted from other regiments for their services or strong family interest. Lieut.-Colonel Coghlan was a smart, experienced officer, very kind to all, but a strict disciplinarian; and as there was no end to our parades, we soon became a most efficient regiment, and the most united and happy corps of officers I ever knew.

CHAPTER 11

Voyage to Barbados

I had the good fortune to see at Portsmouth the Prince Regent of England, the Emperor of Russia, the Emperor of Austria, the King of Prussia, the Duke of Wellington, Marshal Blucher, Marshal Beresford, Lord Hill, Lord Combermere, Prince Esterhazy, Contezoff, and many more distinguished English and foreign officers, all in uniform, and covered with their brilliant stars and orders. This was immediately after the first occupation of Paris and the declaration of peace. It was a glorious day, and all the world was there to see them. A few months afterwards we embarked for Guernsey, and remained there till October of the same year, when we embarked for Barbados.

Our residence in Guernsey was more than usually gay. There were several other regiments of the line stationed there at the same time, and the people of the town and neighbourhood were more than hospitable, for we had constant dinner-parties and public and private balls. The young ladies were more than usually numerous, and very many of them very beautiful. In such a society, and with such luring temptations, it cannot appear a matter of wonder that most of our young men were, or fancied they were, desperately in love; and to encourage our pretensions our kind and ambitious colonel (who was himself a married man) at every ball slyly hinted to the elderly ladies and mothers, as his officers passed near, "That is the nephew or cousin of Lord So-and-so, and "That is a young man of considerable property in the West Indies," and so on, in the most seductive manner, until he made us all out to be men of substance and wealth. How far this marvellous information was believed I know not, but it did not in any way lessen the continued friendship and hospitality which we invariably received.

Every evening after dinner carriages from our friends assembled in front of our mess-room, and as the constant use of these caused many of us to be absent from parades on the following mornings, with the consequent displeasure and reprimand from our colonel, we used to allow them to remain stationary for some time after the appointed hour for our departure, knowing well that our colonel (who lived opposite our mess room) was watching us all the time, and that, although he did pitch into us for being absent from his parades, he was nevertheless as anxious for our enjoyment and fun as we were ourselves; therefore we pretended to show no desire to be off, until this mock indifference brought our kind commander over and in amongst us, saying, Gentlemen, gentlemen, you are late why are you not off?"

On this one of our captains (Parker), who was for many years private secretary to his Royal Highness the Duke of Kent and a man of courteous address, used to get up and say, "Really, colonel, you are very good, but we have determined not to go to any more parties for fear of being late for parades in the morning." Then he would answer, "Pooh, pooh! d—n the parades; you must all go—you must all go." And so we started for our rooms and dressed and were off as usual.

So long were our dancing and parties continued that most of us were again absent from parade the following morning. Our colonel still continued to send sergeants to town to look for us, and to say he wished to see us immediately. Soon after that, Captain Parker followed alone to smooth the way and to prepare for our reception. This he effectually did by his well-timed excuses and his courteous manner, so that when we arrived in barracks the colonel was so perfectly satisfied that he only said he was glad to hear that we enjoyed ourselves so much. This was latterly almost an everyday occurrence, and I mention it here to show how happy young men may be under a good and kind colonel.

But all things must have an end, and so had our fun in Guernsey; for, as I have already said, we all embarked in October for Barbados, leaving our sweethearts and friends without coming to any positive understanding as to the future. On our voyage we called at the Cove of Cork, where we remained for some days, and were then joined by the 40th Regiment in transports, bound for the West Indies and finally for New Orleans, and here our good and much respected friend Colonel Coghlan left us and retired on half-pay.

I was at this time in command of one of our transports, and here must notice an instance of true honesty that occurred. Being tired of visiting the Cove, I agreed with some officers to take a run up to Cork for a day or two; but, before leaving my ship, I gave orders to the senior officer not to allow any of the men to go on shore. On my return to the Cove I met some of the officers, who told me that my servant had deserted, having got leave to land on the pretence of taking my clothes to be washed. This alarmed me not a little, for I had then between three and four hundred pounds belonging to the troops and to myself in one of my trunks, in dollars and doubloons, and as I entrusted my servant, whom I had long known, with my keys, I now made sure all was gone; I hurried on board and found the door of my cabin locked, and, inquiring for the key, an officer handed it to me, saying my man Henry gave it to him with a request to let no one have it except his master, should I return before he did.

I instantly opened my cabin, and the first thing I observed was my bunch of keys hanging by a piece of twine from the top of the berth; I seized them with a trembling hand and heart, and instantly opened the money trunk, and on counting my bags and treasure, to the honour of poor Henry be it told, not one dollar was missing. Poor, honest Henry was never afterwards heard of by me, and I was glad he had secured his escape, for had he been captured and brought back he must have been severely punished.

We finally sailed from the Cove of Cork escorted by a line-of-battle ship and two small men-of-war, and for a day or two made good progress; but we were then caught in a severe gale, right against us, and after struggling for a day or two the sign was made by our commodore to return to "port in view," namely Bantry Bay, on which all the fleet put about, and, led by the line-of-battle ship, steered direct for that safe and splendid anchorage, which is very extensive within, but narrow and dangerous at its entrance, so that not more than one ship can enter with safety at a time.

As we were passing in, one of our fleet, the *Baring* transport, with the 40th Regiment on board, got so near the rocks that she struck, and immediately after went broadside on, and finally became a total wreck. My ship followed in her wake and passed within fifty yards of the stranded vessel, and it being then early in the day, it was most distressing and heart-rending to see the sufferers all in confusion crying for help, which from our position it was quite impossible to render, for we were obliged to run in, in order to save ourselves. So was every other ship as she reached and entered the same narrow passage. But the men-of-war and other vessels which had got safely into the bay soon sent their boats to the rescue, and all the soldiers and crew, excepting about fifteen wretched men, women, and children who were drowned in their hurry to jump on the rocks, were saved, but the ship and nearly all the baggage and cargo were lost.

I remember as we passed the ill-fated ship seeing an officer's wife standing and screaming on the poop, her infant in her arms, and with no covering beyond her nightdress; I heard afterwards that the child fell out of her arms and was drowned, but she herself was saved. The survivors were encamped on the beach for some days, and then were divided for a time amongst the other transports, on which the whole fleet again returned to the Cove of Cork to charter another vessel for the sufferers.

About a week after that we sailed once more for our destination. The weather was fair and beautiful until we arrived off Funchal, in Madeira, and thence we had a dead calm. Some of my brother officers from another ship came on board, and being, as we supposed, close in to the town, we proposed after dinner to go on shore. We had a lieutenant of the navy as agent of transport in charge of us. As he made no objection to our landing (believing the calm would continue until the following morning) our captain consented, and ordered two boats to be manned, so eight of us started on the clear understanding that we should return by daylight next morning. Our sailors, who were promised all sorts of drinks and rewards, pulled most heartily, but the distance to the shore proved much further than we expected, and a dark night overtook us; but still we pushed on, and the brilliant lights in the town cheered us. At last we reached the beach and found a heavy surf running in, and none of us knew the proper place for landing; but the sailors, undaunted, assured us there could be no danger, so one of the boats (not mine) took the lead, and was no sooner in the surf than she was instantly upset and all her passengers were seen struggling in the sea; but after a good ducking they all got safe on shore, and also managed to secure their boat.

My sailors wanted to try the same risk, but I would not allow them. Seeing a shore battery near us, we approached, and were challenged by a Portuguese sentry, and answered, "English officers, who request to be allowed to land." This the sentry refused, and said his orders were to allow no one to land. My knowledge of the language was now of some use to me, and after talking to the sentry quietly and kindly and promising him a dollar, the brave man suffered us at once to step on shore, and showed us the way to the town. There we found our friends, still dripping wet, but with some good wine before them. After refreshing ourselves a little, we went to look after our boats and sailors, and found all safe. We then gave them sufficient money to make them comfortable, and urged them to leave one man at least as sentry over the boats. This they promised to do, so we returned to our hotel, determined to have our fun also. Soon after this the weather from a calm suddenly changed to a strong wind and heavy rain, which continued to pour without any change during the whole night. This damped our follies, but we were up and at our boats before daylight next morning. These we found all safe, but not a sailor to be seen anywhere; and when daylight appeared not one of our ships was in sight. This was truly distressing and alarming, but we had still hopes of seeing and overtaking our fleet, for beyond the town, and in our course, a long promontory of land projected, sufficient to conceal our ships from us, even if they were close behind that obstruction.

Without further delay we searched for our sailors and eventually found them, but in such a state and humour from drink that they positively refused to go to their boats, or any farther with us, saying that we all had been dry and enjoying ourselves, while they were left hungry and wet watching the boats. All our coaxing and entreaties had no effect, and they got worse and worse and even insolent. At last large promises of grog and money when we should reach our ships made some impression on the best of them, and after many more oaths and much grumbling, the others at last consented to go with us, still believing our ships could not be far beyond the distant point. Our next care was (having had no breakfast) to get some cold meat and bread and a couple of kegs of good wine. Our boats were then launched, and off we started with three cheers. It took us two good hours to pull round the point; then came our great fear and alarm, for although the wide ocean was then clear as far as the eye could reach, only one solitary ship was to be seen, and that nearly hull down, in our direct course. Here the sailors again declared they would not go one yard farther. Much conversation and many arguments followed, and for a time we did not know what to do. To go back to Funchal would be our ruin, and risk perhaps our commissions; moreover, all our money was gone, and as we were strangers we did not know where to get more. At last great promises were renewed, and after another and another tumbler of wine our mutinous crew consented to try to make the ship in sight. Fortunately the weather was moderate, and we had a light breeze in our favour; by good luck, also, we had a few empty bags in our boats, which were intended to carry off some vegetables to our ships; with these the sailors managed to rig out some sails fixed upon oars; this assisted them very much in their pulling, yet with all their struggling and endless swearing it was not till four in the afternoon that we managed to reach the ship, which we hoped to be our own, but, alas! we were again disappointed, for she proved to be an American whaler; but we were received most kindly, and provided at once with a good dinner.

From her deck another ship was in sight, about ten miles distant, which the American captain assured us was one of our own convoy, and that he had observed her all day, as our fleet went by, trying to remain as much as possible behind, on the pretence of making repairs. This was cheering, if we could but get our men to take again to their boats. At last we prevailed, and off we started, the American captain giving us a small cask of water and some rum to cheer us; and at seven o'clock that evening, after a trying exposure and fatigue of eleven hours, we reached the sail in sight (which proved to be our ship) in safety, thankful indeed for our escape from the tremendous danger to which we had so foolishly exposed ourselves. Had it come on to blow hard at such a distance from the land, the chances were that we must have perished or been starved to death from want of provisions. When we got on board our fleet was just visible ahead from our decks, and it took us two days under all sail to make up with them.

Chapter 12
St. Vincent and Guadeloupe

There were no less than four more regiments of the line in Barbados at that time, so that each succeeding day we were more and more entertained and fêted. The garrison was then very healthy, and we began to think ourselves in good quarters and the climate not quite as bad as all the world represented it to be. For weeks and weeks we got on very well, and without much sickness. At last a gradual change took place, and we began to lose men daily, and soon the numbers increased, the prevailing complaint being yellow fever, which also attacked the other regiments in garrison. We were the last comers, and lost considerably more than any of the other regiments. Amongst our dead was our paymaster, Captain Thompson. His death occasioned a committee of paymastership to be appointed, of which I was the junior member, and as the others disliked the work, I engaged, with the consent of my commanding officer, to do all, and consequently I got the whole of the allowances, namely, nine shillings per day in addition to my pay. I also continued to do my regimental duties.

About this time I was appointed president of a garrison court-martial. The case was one of much difficulty and complicated evidence, but we got through it, and the proceedings were forwarded to Major-General Robert Douglass (then Adjutant-General to the Forces in the West Indies and commanding the garrison), by whom they were at once approved, and nothing more was heard on the subject till a fortnight later, when, to my surprise, I saw my name in General Orders as deputy judge-advocate-general! I immediately wrote to General Douglass thanking him for the appointment and stating that I should endeavour to fulfil the duties to the best of my powers. On the following morning I received the more than flattering answer as follows:

Sir,

In appointing an officer to perform the important duties of Deputy Judge-Advocate it was my duty to select a competent one, and I am satisfied I have done so.

I have the honour to be, etc., etc., etc.,

Robert Douglass

Major-General and Adjutant-General

The first case for trial in my new appointment was unfortunately that of a captain of my own regiment (for being drunk on duty). He was found guilty and cashiered, but strongly recommended to mercy on account of his former services, and this recommendation from the court induced His Majesty to allow him to retire from the service by the sale of his commission. After this I had occasion to see General Douglass repeatedly, but, as he was a very reserved man and at all times a very strict disciplinarian, I had no intimacy with him then beyond our formal meetings; however, as I shall hereafter show, we became intimate soon afterwards.

The York Chasseurs were removed to the island of St. Vincent, and we had not been many months there under our new Lieut.-Colonel Ewart, when General Orders reached us from headquarters (Barbados) detailing an expedition then ordered from the various islands in the command to be immediately formed to proceed against the islands of Martinique and Guadeloupe, and to rendezvous in the first instance at the small group of islands called the "Saints." The York Chasseurs were included and attached to Major-General Campbell's brigade, and all the staff appointments were filled except that of brigade major. Our senior captain at this time was Holland Daniel, a distant relative of Sir Henry Torrens, then Adjutant-General to His Majesty's Forces at the Horse Guards, and from whom my friend Holland Daniel brought out letters to our Commander-in-Chief, Lieut.-General Sir James Leith, who was also an officer of some service with the 61st Regiment in Spain and Portugal, so that when the General's orders appeared with the staff vacancy which I have named, Captain Holland Daniel made sure he would be the fortunate man to fill it. In a few days our transports arrived, and we embarked and sailed for the appointed rendezvous, and there found a considerable number of troops already arrived; and several ships-of-war, with the admiral and Sir James Leith, and other transports with troops were standing in. As soon as we got to anchor Colonel Ewart went on board the admiral's ship to report his arrival, and on returning in his boat we observed him standing up and waving a paper over his head. We at once believed this to be good news, and on reaching the deck he said "Anderson, you are the lucky man; you were appointed major of brigade, but in justice to myself and my regiment I have been obliged to object to your leaving me, and I have done so, with the assurance to the Commander-in-Chief and to General Douglass, who recommended you, that no one rejoiced more than I at your good fortune, and that I objected to your leaving me solely on the grounds of your being one of the few officers of my regiment who ever saw service, and to whose experience, therefore, I attached the greatest importance, as we were now sure of going into action. I told the Commander-in-Chief that I had the highest opinion of you as an able and intelligent officer, and that I should be willing to part with you when the fight was over should his Excellency then see fit to give you any other staff appointment."

All this was very gratifying, yet very galling, for staff appointments are not so easily had, but I could not do less than thank him for his good opinion and patiently bear my fate. Ewart saw my distress and said: "Come, I must take you on board the flagship and introduce you to the Commander-in-Chief." So off we started, but on getting on board Sir James Leith was so engaged that he could not see me, but General Douglass received us, and Colonel Ewart went again kindly over his objections and said much more to please and flatter me. General Douglass said that I must remain for the present with my regiment, and that he was glad to hear such a good report of me. We then took leave and returned to our own ship.

During that and the following day the whole of the troops of the expedition arrived, and about the same time a frigate came from England bringing the news of the battle of Waterloo, the abdication of Bonaparte, and the restoration of the Bourbon dynasty to the throne of France. This great and astounding news was at once dispatched under a flag of truce by the admiral, Sir Charles Durham, and Sir James Leith to the respective governors of Martinique and Guadeloupe, with the earnest request that they would at once acknowledge and show their loyalty to Louis XVIII, their now reigning King, and thus put an end to our intended hostile proceedings and useless effusion of blood. The governor of Martinique at once acknowledged the sovereignty of the Bourbons, and hoisted the white flag, but General Boyer, of Guadeloupe, returned an answer that he did not believe one word of the news, and that he was determined to fight for his Emperor and to resist to the last.

On the following morning, the 9th of August, 1815, our armament sailed from the Saints in two divisions for

Guadeloupe, the main body of the force under the Commander-in-Chief for Grande Ance Bay, and one brigade, consisting of the 63rd Regiment and York Chasseurs under Major-General Douglass, for Bailiffe. In a few hours the whole were landed in safety at these places respectively. Our landing at Bailiffe was opposed by a considerable number of French infantry, but we had a man-of-war with us, which covered our landing and cleared the beach for a sufficient distance to enable us to get on shore safely. The enemy formed again at a little distance inland, and there we at once attacked them, and finally drove them before us till they reached Basse Terre and got under the protection of the batteries of Fort Matilda, beyond which we took up our position for the night, expecting to be joined by our main body next day. In the course of this day we lost some men, but no officers except Captain Lynch of the 63rd. The main body of our troops was also opposed on landing, and constantly during this march of two days from Grande Ance to Basse Terre, but their casualties were not numerous, and they joined us in safety at the expected time. Guns were then put into position, and they began battering the town, the fire being ably returned from Fort Matilda. Preparations were at the same time made by us for storming, and when the proper time arrived a flag of truce was sent in, giving the enemy the choice of surrendering without risking any further additional loss of life. This the governor refused, but the French general officer, who was next in authority, at once complied. He hauled down the tricolour and hoisted the white flag, acknowledging all as prisoners of war.

The 63rd and some more of our troops marched in and took possession, the French garrison having first marched out under arms and laid them down in front of our main force, which was drawn up in line ready to receive them. The French troops, as prisoners of war, were formed in separate divisions and marched back to town into separate places of confinement until ships were ready to receive them, which finally took them back to France. The officers were allowed to retain their swords, and both they and the men were allowed to keep their private baggage. The governor, General Boyer, was nowhere to be found, till after a long search he was discovered concealed in a wine-cellar, determined to the last to uphold the honour of his Emperor. Of course, he was treated with every kindness, and was sent with the others to France.

A week afterwards the whole of our troops were re-embarked and went back to their former quarters in the different islands, except the 25th Regiment, which was left to garrison Basse Terre and Guadeloupe, and the latter was now made the headquarters of the British troops in the West Indies. I returned with my regiment to St.Vincent and continued my additional duties as acting paymaster, expecting nothing better for some time. In a few weeks the General Orders arrived, and to my great delight and surprise I read: "Captain Joseph Anderson, of the York Chasseurs, to be Deputy-Assistant Quartermaster-General to the Forces, and to repair forthwith to Headquarters, Guadeloupe." I was indeed proud of my extraordinary good luck, and so was Colonel Ewart, and as a mark of his regard he made me a present of a handsome staff sword, which he had himself worn for many years in a similar appointment. I soon handed over my company and my accounts as paymaster to officers appointed for those duties, and availed myself of a passage in the very first vessel that started for Guadeloupe, and arrived there safely.

CHAPTER 13

Dominica

Colonel Popham, of my old regiment, the 24th, was then deputy-quartermaster-general and the head of my department. He was always on the staff, and had not served much with the 24th during my time, so that I was very little known to him; but he received me most kindly, and set me at once to work in his office at correspondence and various public returns, which gave me a good idea of the duties. Thus I continued more than a month, until at last, being considered up to my work, I was sent off to Point à Pitre, thirty miles from Basse Terre, to take the sole charge of that station, or rather of the duties of the department, for there I found Colonel Brown as commandant with his 6th West India Regiment. A more charming man and able officer I have seldom or ever met. I became a member of the mess, which was well conducted and most comfortable. Although we had little society at Point à Pitre, I found enough to do, and spent my time very happily there for some months.

I was then suddenly ordered to hand over my charge to Captain Killy Kelly, of the 6th West India Regiment, and to proceed to Roseau, in the island of Dominica, to take charge of the department there, and I found the change a very agreeable one. The governor at the time, Colonel Maxwell, was a most kind and hospitable man, and I lived within a few yards of Government House. There was a very extensive and pleasant society amongst the residents and settlers in the town of Roseau and its neighbourhood. Parties and dinners were frequent, and I enjoyed them very much; but, alas! our greatest pleasures are subject to change, and ours had a partial check which proved very distressing to many.

I was dining with a large party at Government House, and amongst the guests was a Dr. de Ravière. The conversation turned on foot races, and he boasted much of his powers and success in that line. I had had some experience in running also, and asked him what odds he would give me in a thousand yards. He declined giving any odds, and so we agreed to run equal for two hundred dollars. A place and day was at once appointed. At the given day and hour (three in the afternoon) no less than four thousand people had assembled, lining each side of the road we were to run. Tents and marquees were pitched for our dressing and for refreshments. Amongst the spectators were Dr. de Ravière's two lovely sisters. We soon appeared, both dressed in flannel, and the word being given we started. I allowed him to lead for twenty yards, then pushed on, and for a few yards we ran abreast; then I passed him, increasing my advantage. He (in trying to overtake me) fell down, and became for a time almost insensible. He was carried home and put to bed; fever soon followed, and next day he was dead. In the absence of a medical man a Major Jack undressed me and put me into a tub of rum as a bath, then to bed, giving me a mixture of brandy and porter till I became almost unconscious, and finally fell into a sound sleep, from which I did not awake till next morning. I was free from fever, but was confined to my bed for that and the following day, and was kept ignorant of the fate of Dr. de Ravière for some days longer. It was indeed a foolish frolic to attempt to run a thousand yards in such a climate and at such an hour.

I remained at Roseau for some months after, with an excellent house and good allowances, amounting in all to more than double my regimental pay. Early in 1817 orders arrived from England for the removal of the York Chasseurs from the Windward and Leeward Islands to Jamaica, a distinct and separate command. I was then written to, officially, to say that my staff appointment would be continued if I exchanged into another regiment within that command, but if not I must follow the York Chasseurs to Jamaica in command of a detachment of the regiment still remaining at St. Vincent. This was a serious step for me to decide on, and I took some days before I finally made up my mind. I was then the second captain of my regiment, and to exchange into another would place me at the bottom of the captains, and yet my appointment was a most important and lucrative one, and such as I might never again hope to enjoy. For days I was quite undecided and did not know what to do, but at last I thought the least risk and the best chance of promotion was to give up my appointment and to follow my regiment. I wrote to the adjutant-general (my friend General Douglass) accordingly, and in due course I saw my name in General Orders directing me to hand over the charge of the quartermaster-general's department and to join a detachment of my regiment at St. Vincent.

The first opportunity was from Barbados, from which island I knew I could readily get a passage to St. Vincent. I left Dominica in a small colonial schooner, the Johanna, commanded by a mulatto and manned exclusively by negroes. Our captain knew nothing of navigation, but was in the habit of making this voyage successfully by taking his departure from Point des Salines, in Martinique, and steering direct east, against the trade winds, for a day or two, to clear the islands, and then due south, with a man at the mast-head to look out for Barbados, which is a very high land. In clear weather it is seen at a distance of fifty-nine or sixty miles, but we had thick fogs and much rain, so that though we cruised about with a man constantly at the mast-head for some days, we could nowhere discover the island nor any other land. In despair our captain turned back before the trade winds, sure of making some of the islands, from which he could again take a fresh departure. About sunset we recognized Martinique, and on the following morning Point des Salines once more, from which we again took our departure; but that effort proved worse than the former, for on the second day we were opposed by a fearful hurricane, which carried away both our masts, and left us a helpless, unmanageable hulk in a wild and terrible sea. Our situation became indeed most fearful and alarming. The sea was constantly breaking over us, and wherever there was any opening it rushed in tons below, until the cabin, where I was alone, was completely flooded by many feet of water. All the crew except the captain gave up in despair, and shut themselves up below, crying and moaning all the time. The captain manfully kept to the deck, lashing himself to the tiller ring-bolts. In this perilous situation we continued for two days and one night, expecting every moment to be our last, for our ill-fated barque, being under no control, was tossed about at the mercy of the raging seas.

We gave up all hope—then, recommending ourselves to Providence, we expected every moment to founder. In this awful and long-continued danger I must confess my mind was much troubled about a few hundred pounds which I had on board with me, in doubloons and dollars, and which I sorely grieved to think my sister would now lose. On the second day of this hurricane a sail appeared in sight (or rather a vessel under almost bare poles). It soon passed near us, and our captain managed to show his ensign on a spar upside down, expecting that the stranger would try and come to our assistance; but instead of doing so, he hoisted his own flag reversed, and continued his course. Although this was an English man-of-war, she was in such distress and danger in this heavy gale and raging sea that it was quite impossible for her to come near us or to render any help.

Towards the evening of the following day the storm moderated, and by great exertions our people managed to rig up something like a jury-mast, on which they hoisted one or two of the smaller sails, and we bore away before the trade wind, sure of making some of the islands which we knew must be to leeward. In the evening land was seen ahead, but the sea was still running so high that our captain was afraid to go too near it, and so kept an offing as he best could until next morning. Then at daylight we steered for the land; in a few hours we were satisfied that it was the island of St. Lucia, and about noon we got to the anchorage, with our lives at least in safety, and truly thankful, indeed, for our marvellous escape from death. I took my final leave of the schooner Johanna and landed at once, and here I found my friend General Douglass acting-governor of the island. I dined with him, and on the following day, with his advice, took my passage in a small vessel bound direct for St. Vincent, where I arrived in safety, and took command of the detachment of my regiment, then under orders for Jamaica.

Chapter 14

An Amusing Duel

I had not been many days at St. Vincent before the papers announced that no less than sixteen vessels had foundered in the late hurricane, and as none of the crews were heard of it was taken for granted that they must have all perished. I soon afterwards left St. Vincent with my detachment, and after a pleasant voyage arrived in safety at Port Royal, Jamaica. On the following day I landed and joined the headquarters of my regiment at Stony Hill barracks. The change from staff to regimental duties I did not much like, but there was no help for it. I found myself again associated with my gay and happy brother officers, with Major Dumas in command, Colonel Ewart having gone on leave. Some months afterwards four companies of the regiment were detached and sent under my command to Falmouth, Montego Bay, Marroon Town, and Savanna-la-mar, my station being at the former of these places. Our barracks there and at all the other stations were very good and we enjoyed ourselves very much. For nearly two years we were quartered in that part of Jamaica. My orders were to visit each detachment occasionally, which I did repeatedly, not solely as a point of duty, but also for my own amusement.

About the month of March, 1818, our senior major arrived from England and took command of the regiment at Stony Hill; Major Dumas joined us at Falmouth, and relieved me of my charge. I now began seriously to think of a trip to England, for my health was not particularly good and I required a change. On consulting our assistant-surgeon, he advised me to apply for a medical board, so I wrote officially to Major Dumas, who forwarded my application to the deputy adjutant-general at headquarters, Kingston, and by return of post I was advised to repair to Stony Hill, to appear before a medical board. I made that journey, a hundred and twenty miles overland, on horseback in four days. I appeared before the board, who, without asking me any questions, recommended me for twelve months' leave of absence to England. We sailed from Port Royal early in April, and touched at Havana, where we remained ten days, shipping at night (contrary to the laws of the port but with the connivance of the governor) thousands and thousands of dollars and doubloons on account of merchants in England, upon which our admiral and his senior officer had a large percentage. We left Havana, and arrived in England early in May, 1818, after a most agreeable passage. The admiral and his captain were particularly jolly, and very kind to us all; the former had the officers of the wardroom daily at dinner in their turn, and entertained us with his numerous stories; among other things he told us he had made a hundred thousand pounds during his three years' command on the Jamaica station.

Again in England, and with my health much improved by the voyage, I endeavoured to enjoy myself as much as I could. About December, 1819, I heard that the York Chasseurs were ordered from Jamaica to Canada, to be there disbanded, consequent upon the general peace which followed the battle of Waterloo and the great reductions in the British army. Soon afterwards I received an official letter informing me that I was to consider myself on half-pay in three months from that date. This was indeed bad and most unexpected news for me, but I endeavoured to make the best of it, consoling myself with the hope of getting employed again as soon as possible by an appointment to some other regiment, and in this mind I returned soon afterwards to London, determined to see what chances I had at the Horse Guards. After waiting some time I attended the levée of the Military Secretary, Lieut.-General Sir Henry Torrens, and stated my case, and my anxiety to be employed. He received me with his usual consideration and kindness, and directed me to write to him on the subject. I did so in due course, and soon received his answer saying that on my stating my readiness to proceed to Sierra Leone I should be appointed to a company of the 2nd West India Regiment. I immediately wrote back saying that my health was still very indifferent, from my services in the West Indies, but that rather than forfeit all hopes of employment I would proceed to Sierra Leone, should his Royal Highness the Commander-in-Chief wish me to do so. This was a decision forced on me, and anything but satisfactory to my feelings, so with fear and trembling I watched every succeeding gazette which appeared for the next month, expecting to see myself appointed to the 2nd West India Regiment, but to my joy no such notice appeared then or afterwards, and I again began to breathe freely and hope for something better.

Months of idleness passed in London, and as I was afraid to appeal again to the Horse Guards for a time, I determined to go at once to France to study the language, for I well remembered how much inconvenience I had suffered while in the French island of Guadeloupe from not being able to speak French fluently. Fortunately, at this time I was in correspondence with a dear friend and brother officer, Lieutenant Wharton of the York Chasseurs, and I persuaded him to accompany me to France. Having made our arrangements, we left London early in 1820 for Southampton, where we took our passages in a sailing mail packet for Jersey, and from thence to St. Malo in Brittany, and there, for the first time, I found myself in "*la belle France.*" Next morning we went up the St. Malo river, in a passage boat, for about twenty miles to Dinan, and having procured good lodging, we remained there for nearly a month, then started on foot, determined to make easy stages in the same way until we reached Nantes. After our second day's travelling we found ourselves tired and done up, so we rested a day, and on the following morning took our seats in the diligence direct for Nantes. Here we managed to get most comfortable lodgings with a widow named Fleury and her two pretty daughters, who provided us with our breakfast in our own English fashion. We became members of a most excellent *table d'hôte*, where we met many French officers belonging to the regiment then in garrison, and with whom we soon became intimate, for we told them we were officers, and had had the honour of having been opposed to them.

In February, 1821, I returned to London, stopping for a few days *en route* with a friend at Boulogne-sur-Mer. This was Dr. McLaughlin, whom I knew in Portugal as a staff assistant-surgeon, who attended me while sick at Lisbon. His name being now before me, reminds me of him as a gay young fellow who, one morning at Lisbon, went to visit another assistant staff surgeon named McDermot, who was not at home when he called, but he saw his landlady, a handsome young widow, and, if the account be true, he attempted to kiss her; at least, so she told her lodger on his return home. McDermot at once called on McLaughlin and begged him to make her an apology. This he refused, saying he took no improper liberties, and saw no necessity whatever for an apology, and laughed at the very idea of being asked to make one. They were good friends and spoke and argued at first as such, but soon they both got very angry and excited, and McLaughlin, having a whip in his hand, forgot himself, and actually struck the other more than once with it, and then told him he was ready to give him any satisfaction he required. Dr. McDermot then left him, and McLaughlin came to me and told me the whole story, and that he, of course, expected a challenge at once, and begged I would go out with him, as his friend.

I was then lying in bed, far from well, but I consented on the understanding that he would allow me to use my own discretion in all and every way. While we were talking, the hostile message was brought by an officer, an Irishman, whom I found very stubborn and unreasonable then and afterwards; we talked over the affair, and I used my best endeavours to try and bring the matter to an amicable conclusion, admitting that my friend had committed himself most seriously, and was truly sorry for what he had done, and was ready and anxious to make the most ample apology; but the Irishman would not hear of anything less than a meeting, and said that nothing less would satisfy his friend or himself. It was finally settled that they should meet at a given place next morning, and with this understanding the obstinate Irishman left me. I now sent for McLaughlin and told him all that had passed, and that he must be prepared to go with me at the appointed hour next morning. He was quite cool and collected, and then left me, as he said, to arrange his papers and settle his affairs. He afterwards told me he was so employed during the best part of the night, and he also gave me certain instructions in case of anything happening to him. We kept our engagement punctually, and we found the others waiting for us with a medical man in attendance. After some talk and a toss up, it fell to my lot to measure the ground (twelve paces), to see the principals into their places, and to give the word or signal to fire; but I had previously told McLaughlin to allow McDermot to fire first, then to fire his own pistol in the air, thus showing he had given his adversary the chance to shoot him, and by this action admitting himself to be in the wrong; all this my friend agreed to, and promised to do.

When they had taken their places I asked, "Are you ready?" and on being answered "Yes," I said, "Present," and so kept them for a few seconds, when I dropped my handkerchief as the signal to fire. McDermot fired and missed my friend, who instantly afterwards fired his pistol in the air. I stepped forward to McDermot's friend and said, "Gentlemen, I hope you are satisfied?" The Irishman answered, "Certainly not, they must go on." I endeavoured in vain to convince him that the rules of honour were satisfied, that his friend had had the chance of shooting mine, and that mine had fully acknowledged himself in the wrong by firing his pistol in the air. Dr. McDermot appeared to agree with me, but said he must leave all to his second; but the Irishman became more and more excited, and said he could not be satisfied until they had another shot or two. I then said, "Well, sir, it must be you and I to go on, for I cannot suffer these gentlemen to go any further; so come on." This worked a marvellous change, and my brave Irish boy soon became cool and reasonable; finally, we all shook hands and returned to Lisbon, and had a comfortable breakfast together in a café. This was the first and only duel I ever was concerned in, and yet in my early days duels and hard drinking were frequent evils, and considered by many to be both necessary and unavoidable.

CHAPTER 15

Chased by a Pirate

In April, 1821, I again attended the Commander-in-Chief's Military Secretary's levée. Sir Henry Torrens was still in office, and when I told him of my anxiety to be employed he asked me where I would like to serve. I said, "Jamaica above all other parts of the world"; he then directed me to write to him to that effect. I did so next day, and three weeks afterwards had the pleasure of seeing myself appointed captain of a company in the 50th Regiment, and I soon received an official letter advising me to join the depot of the regiment in the Isle of Wight, which I did in the month of July following. I remained doing duty there for nearly twelve months, and it was during that period that I had a severe attack of inflammation of the eyes, which induced me to appeal to Lord Palmerston for the second, and last time, for my pension.

We embarked for Jamaica in the hired ship *Echo*, but were detained by contrary winds in Cowes harbour for a fortnight. The captain had his wife on board during our detention, and we were so much pleased with his manner and polite attentions that we invited him to become our guest during the voyage (for in those days officers so embarked provided their own messing), and all went on well until a fine fair wind enabled us to sail: the captain then landed his wife, and from that hour and for ten days after he was never sober.

During this time the mate took charge, but in a few days we were met by a fearful gale right against us, and every hour and day it became worse and worse. Our captain still remained beastly drunk and most troublesome, every now and then throwing handfuls of silver, and some gold, amongst the soldiers on deck, allowing them to scramble for it, and when spoken to by any of us, swearing and damning and calling out that we were all going to Davy Jones's locker together.

The gale at last increased to a hurricane; the captain then became so troublesome that the senior officers present (Captain Powell and I) went officially to our commanding officer, Colonel P——, and advised him to confine the captain to his cabin, and to order the mate to take the ship back to port, as the sailors were already done up and grumbling. Colonel P—— was a good and kind man, but without energy or resolution, and he declined to interfere or to take any such responsibility on himself. We urged and urged our request, as the lives of all were in danger, but still finding Colonel P—— would not do anything, we insisted on having his leave to act, so that we might ourselves carry out his orders. He then said, "Well, boys, just do as you like."

We then at once forced the captain off the deck into his cabin, and told him he must consider himself under arrest. He got very violent, and swore he would not be kept a prisoner by any one. Then we got him down again and placed two sentries in his cabin, with orders not to suffer him to go on deck. We next went to the mate and told him that his captain was a prisoner for habitual drunkenness and neglect of duty, and that he (the mate) should at once take the ship into port. This the honest sailor refused to do; he could not, he said, act without his captain's orders, that he would be dismissed by the owners and ruined if he did so.

We reported accordingly to Colonel P——, who at once declined further responsibility. The gale continued without any visible change; many of our sails were blown away, the weather became very thick and dirty, our sailors were done up and discontented to a man, yet the mate would do nothing. He confessed the crew were overworked, but that he could not help it, and dared not go back. In this state we got through another day and night, and next morning found ourselves at daylight all but on shore on the island of Alderney, with only enough sea room to clear the rocks ahead of us, on which we must have been wrecked, had not the morning's dawn happily come in time to save us.

When clear in the open sea, we again urged the mate to bear away for the nearest harbour, but he still refused, urging his former reasons. We then begged him to parade the whole crew on the quarter-deck, that we might know their opinions. This he did, and the gallant fellows to a man declared they could not possibly work any longer, and urged us, for the safety of all, to put up in some harbour. For days we had made no observations, but being satisfied it was the island of Alderney we saw that morning the mate had no doubt of our whereabouts. We now went to Colonel P—— (who seldom left his cabin, for he had his wife and a young lady, Miss C——, with him), and we urged or rather insisted upon his signing a written order which we had prepared, directing the mate at once to take the ship back to the nearest port, telling Colonel P—— at the same time the danger we had escaped, and the result of our parade of the crew. As before, he resisted for some time all responsibility, but at last we got him to sign the order. Then followed difficulties with the mate, and it was not until we threatened to put a sentry over him that he consented, and gave the order to bear away and steer for Torbay. At four on the same evening land was reported ahead, and by sunset we were close in, and hoisted a signal of distress, which soon brought us a pilot boat, which boarded us and at once took us safely to anchor, thankful for our escape from destruction.

I now recommended Colonel P—— to report all that had occurred to us to the different authorities in London, and to state the necessity which obliged him to take all the responsibility and to act as he did. Poor man! he became more than ever confused, and said that he would be ruined and brought to a court-martial. I tried all I could to convince him, and he asked me to write the reports in his name, and said that he would sign them if I did so. I dispatched them at once, for fear of his altering his mind, and he soon received an answer approving of all he had done, and thanking him for his most able and judicious conduct.

On the same day the owners came down from London, bringing another captain with them. It was then found that the ship had suffered much, and carpenters and shipwrights were sent from the dockyard at Plymouth to examine and repair her. The owners were so pleased with the assistance which the soldiers gave the sailors during the gale, that they made the former a present of two tons of potatoes. It took more than a fortnight before the *Echo* was again reported fit for sea. During that time we amused ourselves landing and making excursions daily to different parts of the country, and in this interval Colonel P—— had a second letter, saying that our application for additional allowances for our losses during the storm was under favourable consideration; this enabled us to replenish our sea-stock, and to make due provision for our future comfort. We sailed again with a fair breeze, and in due course reached Madeira, where we remained for some days, landing frequently and enjoying ourselves much in that gay town.

From Madeira we soon got into the trade winds, and had delightful sailing, without any extraordinary occurrence, till we got off the island of St. Christopher, when one morning the captain came and roused us all from our beds, saying we were being chased by a pirate. This was startling news, for we had heard that these seas were full of pirates, and that they seldom showed mercy to any one. Our ladies and soldiers' wives began crying and moaning at once, for they expected nothing less than our utter destruction. Most of us hurried on deck in our night-dresses, and there saw a clipper brig bearing down upon us under all sail, about fifteen miles distant. Our captain still trusted that she might be a man-of-war, but when she fired a gun there was no doubt of her being a pirate. We returned in great excitement to our cabins and dressed with all dispatch. I then, as the next senior officer, went to Colonel P—— to report our situation, and to request his orders as to what we ought to do, and begged him to come up at once. His wife got alarmed, and he merely said he could do nothing; but at last told me, "Just do as you like." I returned on deck and consulted with the captain, who observed that it was useless to attempt to run away, as the stranger was gaining fast upon us, and had fired another gun to bring us to. Although we had about ten officers on board and about two hundred soldiers, all these were recruits, and we had not one stand of arms belonging to the troops nor to the ship. However, we decided to make some appearance, and ordered the soldiers to dress in their red coats and caps, to remain ready below, but not to move, till ordered on deck. Meantime the captain furled every sail, except his three top-sails, and with these and his colours flying he continued running easily before the wind. We could clearly see with our glasses the well-known pirates' flag, blue with a white death's-head, flying from the fore top-mast head and the decks crowded with men. Captain Fraser determined to continue our course till the pirate was all but on board of us, then to bring our ship sharp round to the wind, and our men to run up and show themselves in line under our bulwarks, with the officers flourishing their swords, to show we were all ready for action, expecting by this sudden manoeuvre that the pirate would be right aboard or alongside of us before he had time to take in his crowd of sails, and, if so, that we might then have a chance of grappling and boarding him, when our numbers might give us some advantage; but we were no sooner round and brought to the wind than our adversary, as if by magic, had all his extra sails down, and was round to the wind as soon as we were, showing a splendid broadside of nine guns and a crew of no less than eighty men.

We were now within a few hundred yards of each other, and expected every minute a shot amongst us. Nothing was done for about ten minutes; the pirate then lowered his boat, and sent her fully manned to board us. Our captain said she must come to our leeside, and that our only chance was to secure them. This we agreed to do, and at once to dress one of their men in one of our sailor's clothes and to hang him up at our peak, so as to make the pirate believe that his men had taken possession of our ship.

This was a desperate resolution, but as we expected no quarter from them we had no choice but to make the most of our perilous situation. Just as the boat came under our stern a signal of recall was made from the pirate, and the boat at once returned to the brig. We continued to look with additional anxiety, expecting every moment to see the boat come back, but for another ten minutes nothing was done, and our captain then ordered our ship to bear away and continue our course, so as to see what the pirate would do, and whether he would fire and bring us up again. But he thought better of it and allowed us to continue our course in peace, seeing no doubt that we were only troops and that he could not expect much booty from us. During the whole of this time Colonel P–––– never left his cabin. His wife was crying and sobbing the whole time, and all his endeavours were to comfort her. Of the officers then present, only General Gallaway and myself are now living, and on that occasion Gallaway proved himself to be a promising young soldier, for he volunteered to lead the first boarders, should we succeed in grappling with the pirate.

We reached Port Royal in Jamaica a week afterwards, and at once reported our adventures to the admiral, Sir Edward Owen, and from the description our captain gave of the pirate our naval officers knew him well, and had often given him chase in vain. Two or three men-of-war were now sent to look for him, but returned in a few days without seeing him. Dozens of pirates, of various classes, were at this time cruising in these seas, and had made many captures, plundering and burning their prizes, and barbarously ill-treating and murdering their victims. We had a large naval force on the Jamaica station at this time, and they captured many of these lawless pirates, who were at once tried, and in every instance found guilty and sentenced to be hanged. I attended some of the trials and saw many of these daring fellows, who were plucky to the last, for they did not deny but actually gloried in their calling. They were men of all nations, but principally Italians and Spaniards. We landed on the following day at Kingston, and our different detachments of officers and men joined their respective regiments, viz., the 33rd, 50th, and 92nd.

The English mail which left England after us arrived at Port Royal some time before we did, and Colonel P—— found a letter waiting for him from the Secretary of War authorizing him to draw £80 as compensation for lost sea-stock during the gale already recorded. He therefore called a meeting of the officers who arrived in the *Echo*, and on our assembling read the letter, and proposed dividing the money amongst us, claiming three shares for himself—that is, for himself, his wife, and Miss C——. I said, "No, colonel; you only subscribed one share of our additional expenses, and you may remember that when we agreed to purchase extra provisions at Torbay we, the officers, declined to allow Mrs. P—— or Miss C—— to contribute one shilling to that expense."

On this he got very angry and said, "Well, Captain Anderson, I'll bring you to a court-martial for attempting to obtain money under false pretences."

I answered, "Very well, sir; I believe you signed these letters."

He was thus settled, and most completely put about, and then said, "By G——! I think you are right"; so ended our dispute, and the money was divided share and share alike to each of us.

Chapter 16

Life in Jamaica

Major-General Henry Conran commanded in Jamaica at this time, and the billet of deputy judge-advocate being vacant by the death of Captain Tonge, the general, knowing that I had formerly held this position, at once appointed me to the office. This gave me additional work, and considerable increase of pay. About a year afterwards Major-General Sir John Keane succeeded General Conran, and he retained me still in the appointment. As he was a most uncertain man, my work was trebled, for he never hesitated to bring officers and men to court-martial, even for the most trifling offences. Here, in justice to myself, I must notice that I often told him so, but all to no purpose, for he was always obstinate, and would have his own way.

I may give one instance. Some officers of the 90th had met together one evening in one of the rooms, and two of them got into an altercation, followed by strong and improper language, which induced the senior officers present to place them both under arrest and to report them next morning to their commanding officer, Major Charlton. He ordered a court of inquiry at once before himself in the mess room. Among the witnesses then examined was the paymaster, Captain Micklejohn, a truly noble fellow, who stated all he could remember of what took place on the previous night between the offending officers. He then left the room, but on getting outside and talking to some other officers (who were waiting to be examined) and stating the substance of his evidence to Major Charlton, one of them remarked, "But did you say so and so?" "Oh no, I entirely forgot that, but I shall instantly go back and state it." Micklejohn then begged to be allowed to add to his former evidence, but his commanding officer would not hear him, and desired him to retire. The offending officers, Major W—— and Ensign P——, were brought to general court-martial, and both were found guilty and sentenced to be cashiered. The sentences were approved by his Majesty, but in consideration of former services and the recommendation of the court they were ordered to be severely reprimanded and to return to their duty.

My reason for writing all this is that before the same general court-martial Paymaster Micklejohn was arraigned for conduct unbecoming an officer and a gentleman, in withholding, at a court of inquiry by his commanding officer, evidence which he afterwards gave on oath before a general court-martial. I was the judge-advocate on these trials, and I used every endeavour and argument to convince Sir John Keane and Major Charlton of the injustice and cruelty of bringing an officer, and one of known character, to public trial on such charges, especially as he had returned voluntarily to his commanding officer at once, to offer the evidence which he had forgotten at the moment, thus proving that he did not willingly nor with any intention of screening the offenders withhold his evidence in the first instance. I also pressed upon them the difficulty, nay, the impossibility, for them to repeat word for word the conversation during our own interview; but all was to no purpose: they would not listen to reason, and so they determined he must be tried, and exposed to all the disgrace and annoyances of a general court-martial. He was tried, and the inquiry clearly showed that he did give evidence on oath before a general court-martial which he did not give at the court of inquiry. But it was distinctly proved that he did willingly, and at once, return with a free offer of that evidence, which was declined by his commanding officer. The court therefore found him guilty of not giving the full evidence before the court of inquiry which he gave before the general court-martial, but, under the circumstances which were so clearly shown as to the cause of the omission, the court acquitted the prisoner of all blame, though he was to be slightly reprimanded. This was no more than we all expected, and I told Sir John Keane before the trial that this and this only could be the end of it. I could name other instances equally frivolous and provoking; it is sufficient to say that very many others suffered through him in much the same way.

For the first two years of this my second visit to Jamaica I enjoyed very good health, and yet we had a considerable amount of sickness amongst the troops generally, and several of my friends of the good ship *Echo* died. As far as keeping away from the influence of the sun and living very temperately, of course I took every care of myself. Towards the close of the second year the negroes got very troublesome and insolent to their masters on the north side of the island, and on one or two occasions attempted to commit murder at a station called Port Maria. A company was generally, and for years, stationed at this place, but in consequence of the unusual mortality amongst the troops they were for some months withdrawn, and the barracks were deserted and allowed to fall into decay.

During the above troubles the proprietors and inhabitants of Port Maria made repeated applications to the governor, the Duke of Manchester, for a detachment, and his Grace referred their application to Sir John Keane; but the latter resisted on the plea that the station was considered by the chief medical officers so unhealthy as to be totally unfit for European soldiers, and, in proof of this, repeated how constant and great was the mortality on every former occasion when troops were stationed there. The inhabitants then said that the sickness and deaths which had taken place were all owing to the men being allowed to wander about the country and to get drunk at all hours. These statements and appeals were at last listened to by Sir John Keane, and he ordered a captain, two subalterns, and fifty picked, sober men from my regiment to be at once embarked for Port Maria, with a medical officer. This order was instantly carried out, and I was the unfortunate captain named for this duty. The morning for our embarkation I was sent for by Sir John Keane, who gave me the most strict orders about keeping my men constantly employed by drills and marching out in the mornings, and in the barracks during the days as much as possible, and above all I was to keep them away from all chances and temptations of drinking. He impressed upon me that I could have no excuse for intemperance or irregularities, as all my men were picked and sober soldiers from the different companies of the regiment. He desired me further to report to him by every day's post the state and health of my detachment.

All the previous reports we heard of this place damped our courage from the first, and both officers and men considered our present duties and chances very much like those of a forlorn hope; but on finding our barracks newly done up and painted, and in every way most comfortable, our fears almost vanished, and every succeeding day for a fortnight found us all more and more contented, so much so that we began to wish we might be allowed to remain there as long as we were to serve in Jamaica. In this mind and spirit I continued my daily reports to Sir John Keane, showing that we had not a man in hospital, and the men and officers were most happy and contented. We really were so, though our only society was the Rev. Mr. —— and his family. With him I spent many happy hours, for I soon discovered that during the Peninsular War he was one of the Duke of Wellington's principal spies, with the rank of captain in the army, although he never joined a regiment in his life. He was by birth a German, spoke many languages, and was a most intelligent man and a good and sincere Christian. It was very difficult to make him speak of his former exploits, but when he did he told us wonderful tales of several marvellous hairbreadth escapes in all kinds of characters and disguises, and I know from all reports that he was one of the most efficient and successful spies. After the Peace of 1815 many half-pay officers studied for the Church and took holy orders, and this reverend gentleman was amongst the number.

Up to this time the weather was dry and beautiful, but heavy rains then followed, and continued for a week or more. Our barracks were situated on a high neck of land projecting some distance into the sea, and on our right there was a large mangrove swamp, almost dry until the rains commenced. Then, filling from the hills and valleys to overflowing, it suddenly burst towards the sea, carrying all before it, and from that hour the stench became so powerful that we were all obliged to keep our handkerchiefs to our noses, and so save ourselves as much as possible from its fearful and disgusting effects. From the very first hour of this escape of water, mud, and decayed vegetable matter the whole air became actually poisonous, and our poor men fell sick daily, and in most cases they died before the following day. Some were carried off a few hours after they were attacked, amongst these my own servant, who attended us in good health at breakfast and was dead and buried at night.

I continued well and able to attend to my duties, and by each post reported our sufferings and losses to the Commander-in-Chief. Then, after losing nearly half of my detachment, I received an order to hold all in readiness to embark on the shortest notice to return to headquarters at Kingston, leaving such sick men as could not be removed in charge of our medical officer. This good news I made known at once, and it was received with three cheers. Next morning a smart clipper was seen standing in for our anchorage, and I instantly sent one of my officers down to the landing-place with instructions to wave his hat as soon as a boat came on shore, if he heard the vessel was for us. We watched him with all eyes and the deepest anxiety, and as the boat landed up went his hat; three loud cheers followed from us, and I at once gave orders for immediate parade and embarkation. In half an hour all who could move were on parade, and with our baggage packed ready to move off. On wheeling the detachment back into sections and giving the words "Quick march!" agonizing cries and screams (which I can never forget) were faintly heard from the few poor sick men who were left behind in hospital. There were seven of these unfortunates, and all urged the doctor to allow them to go with the others, saying they would run all risks and would prefer death before reaching the beach, rather than be deserted and left to die there; but the medical officer saw they were too weak to be removed, and tried to comfort them by saying that he himself ran the same risk by remaining with them. We left them, indeed, with great sorrow, and in less than an hour we were safely embarked on board the *Mandeville* and off for Port Royal. Our happy escape from Port Maria, the change of scene and air, soon restored our men to their usual health; but it was very different with the poor fellows left behind, for we heard that three of the number soon died; the remaining four joined us later. I afterwards heard that the barracks at Port Maria were burnt and levelled to the ground by the Government.

CHAPTER 17

Home Again and Married

I remained doing duty in Jamaica for some weeks longer, but began to get anxious to get home, and latterly my health became indifferent. In February, 1825, I applied for a medical board, which recommended me for a year's leave of absence, and with this prospect my health began to improve. The Government decided to send home a number of invalid soldiers, and I was commanded to take charge of them. I was not sorry, for by this chance I was allowed a free passage home. There were several other officers who were also going home on sick leave in the *Speake*. In all there were about two hundred men, a few women and children, and an assistant-surgeon.

We sailed on the 6th of March, and all went well till the night of the 9th, when, with a beautiful clear moon shining, we suddenly ran aground on the outer coral rock of the small and low island of Magna. Fortunately the night was calm, so that we were running not more than three or four miles an hour. The full moon gave us nearly the light of day, and before sunrise we could see the island low but distinctly above the horizon, and then our captain changed our course to steer clear of the land, but the currents must have got hold of us; yet it seemed to me the captain and his chief officer were much to blame, for they were both actually walking the deck when she struck, and had been there for hours before in a clear night. Had there been a proper look out no such accident ought to have taken place. We, the passengers, were all asleep at the time, but the sudden shock and bump of striking roused us all instantly. Officers, soldiers, and women rushed at once without dressing on deck, where the confusion and screaming for some minutes became fearful; but the captain and agent assured us that there was land in front of us and that come what may we need not be alarmed for our lives, as we could all be landed with safety. Meanwhile two of the boats were lowered and carried our anchors astern, and with hawsers from these we tried to work the ship off the rocks into deep water, and my endeavours were equally pressing to clear the decks and to get all who were not wanted for work to go below. It was not till I went down with them and pledged my word to all that I should not leave the ship until the very last man of my charge was landed that I got them all to obey me.

Order was then so far restored, and from over the ship's side we could distinctly see the coral rocks upon which we were fixed, and soon afterwards, from the violent bumping, parts of our copper and sheathing got detached. The low, sandy island, without tree or other vegetation, was within a few hundred yards of us, and every possible effort was continued to heave her off, but all to no purpose. The boats and anchors were then moved first off one quarter and then off the other, and in each of these positions the heavy pulls and straining moved her head and stern round a little. It was then clearly shown that she was fixed as on a pivot in the centre, from which no efforts could move her. The pumps were then tried, and she was found to be making a little water, but not sufficient to cause any unnecessary alarm. At the critical moment it was ascertained that the tide must soon flow inwards, and as both crew and troops were fairly done up it was determined to wait patiently for the tide, when, if the ship made no water, she would be sure to float off. Meantime preparations were made for landing a quantity of provisions and water in case of necessity, and the officers and men packed their portmanteaux and knapsacks ready to make the best of the island of Magna if obliged to land there. About four in the morning the tide began to make, and by six the good ship was afloat again. She was then towed by the boats into deep water and the anchors let go, the pumps tried, and a strict examination made into our condition, when it was found that the leak and water had increased. For some time the captain and agent were undecided whether to continue the voyage or to return to Port Royal, but after waiting for a couple of hours they determined to pass a sail under the ship's bottom and haul it as tight as it could be made, and then to continue the voyage to England. This was done, and we were again steering our way with a fair wind and fine weather. It was well for us that our vessel was built of teak, which enabled her to stand the bumping and thumping, which would at once destroy most ships. We now had New Providence Island before us in our course, in case of being obliged to seek shelter, but all went well till we got off Bermuda, when we were overtaken by a strong gale and heavy sea. The ship laboured much, and the men at the pumps discovered that the water had increased, but as the wind was off the land we had no choice but to run on for England. The pumps kept going during the days and nights. Our commander and our agent showed the best example by their constant watching and exertions; we soon began to lose all our fears in the sure hope of a speedy voyage and a happy end to our troubles, and in another fortnight we were safely anchored at Spithead.

  Our arrival was reported to the authorities in London, and orders came down directing us to proceed without delay to Sheerness. I got leave to land and go to London, on the understanding that I should on the following day go to Sheerness, there to await the arrival of my charge and proceed with them to Fort Pitt, Chatham, and so to deliver them, and their accounts, to the authorities at that station. I applied to General Thornton for leave of absence, but this was flatly refused, until he was satisfied and could report favourably on the state of my depot. Soon afterwards I had the chance of repeating verbally my desire for leave of absence, but as usual he refused, saying it would be a pity to leave my depot for some time longer, as they were getting on so well. I then told him frankly that I was engaged to be married for some time past; that he had obliged me twice already to put it off, and to break my word and my faith; that if he did so any longer my character and my honour must suffer.

On this he laughed heartily and said, "This alters matters; of course, you must go immediately. Send me your application, but you need not wait for an answer—you may start at once."

By that night's post I wrote to my beloved one, told her my difficulties were passed, and that I hoped to be with her soon after she received my letter, and that she alone could now complete my happiness. Three days more found me in London, received with open arms, and lodged in Park Street. A fortnight was allowed to make the necessary dresses and preparations, then my happiness was made perfect. I was married on the 25th November, 1826, at St. Pancras Church, London, to Miss Mary Campbell, only daughter of Colonel Alexander Campbell, by the Rev. Joseph Brakenbury.

In the August following his Royal Highness the Duke of Clarence, as Lord High Admiral of England, visited Portsmouth and honoured the 50th Regiment by presenting us (on Southsea Common, in presence of all the troops in garrison) with new colours, accompanied by a most flattering speech. After the review his Royal Highness, the Duchess of Clarence, and the Colonel-in-Chief, General Sir James Duff, and many of the county families of Hampshire, were entertained at a luncheon in Portsmouth by the officers of the regiment. Lady Duff and my dear wife had the honour of receiving our guests, and about three hundred sat down.

I must here mention a remarkable instance of his Royal Highness's memory. On his arrival at Portsmouth I was introduced to him by General Sir James Lyons, commanding the garrison, and on mentioning our wish that he should do us the honour to present our new colours he said, "Yes, I shall be very happy; I know the history of your regiment quite well, but you may bring me a memorandum on a card of the different actions it has been in."

Next morning I returned to his Royal Highness with a neatly written card showing the battles in which the regiment had been engaged, commencing with Minden, August, 1759. Looking at it, he said, "Sir, you had not a man at Minden; your regiment was then quartered at Haslar barracks."

I answered, "I beg your Royal Highness's pardon, but we always thought our regiment, or some portion of it, was at Minden, and I have myself seen an old breast-plate with the word 'Minden' on it, but I will have another card made out and omit the word."

"Quite unnecessary," he said, and, taking his pen, he scratched it out. I then observed that a very old gentleman who was once in the regiment was then living near Portsmouth, and that I would go and see him, as he might perhaps give me some information on the subject. I took my leave and returned to barracks, and told my colonel and the other officers about my conversation with his Royal Highness; they all laughed, and maintained that our flank companies were at Minden, and urged me to go at once and see old Captain Thompson. I found him, and he in like manner maintained that our flank companies were at Minden.

I returned in triumph, fully believing that his Royal Highness was wrong, and on waiting on him next day I mentioned my interview with Captain Thompson; but again he said, "No, no; you had not a man there," so I took my leave to prepare for the morrow's parade.

We decided on writing to the Army Agents, Messrs. Cox & Co., begging them to go at once to the War Office and request an immediate inspection of the public returns of that period, and of the troops employed at the battle of Minden. In due course we received their answer stating that we had not a man of the 50th Regiment there. His Royal Highness remained at Portsmouth ten days longer, and was entertained daily during that time.

We embarked in a steamer at Liverpool on the 29th June, 1830, and landed on the following forenoon at Dublin. Next morning the 50th Regiment marched in two divisions, headquarters and six companies, under Colonel Woodhouse, for Waterford, and four companies under my command to Clonmel, and in a few months we moved on to Templemore, with detachments at Thurles and Roscrea; and here we enjoyed ourselves very much, Sir Henry Garden and other residents in the neighbourhood having shown us every attention. I was for some time in command of the regiment at Templemore, and it was here that I first had the honour of forming the acquaintance of Lieut.-General Sir Hussey Vivian (afterwards Lord Vivian), who then came to us on a tour of inspection, and who expressed himself much pleased with the regiment.

He was very fond of introducing field movements of his own, and on this occasion asked me to "change front from open column to the rear on a centre company." I told him there was no such movement in the book—but that I would at once do it. He said, "Stop, until I explain it to you."

I begged he would not, but allow me to proceed, and without hesitation I ordered the right centre company to wheel on its centre to the rear, the left wing to go to the right about, and then ordering the right centre company to stand fast, and all the others to form line on that company, by right shoulders forward, the left wing halting and fronting by companies, as they got into the new line, followed by independent file firing from the centre, and by each company as they got into the new alignments, supposing this sudden change of front to be occasioned by the unexpected appearance of an enemy from a wood in our former rear. This fire was kept up for some time, and then we charged the supposed enemy and carried all before us.

Sir Hussey was much pleased, and when our manoeuvring was over he ordered me to form the regiment into hollow square, and then addressed us, and complimented me very much, saying I was the first commanding officer who at once took up his ideas of providing against a sudden surprise from an enemy, and that he "should not fail to make a special report of my efficiency." And I know that afterwards he did so, and that when he got next day to Birr barracks, to inspect the 59th Regiment, he called upon the colonel of that regiment to do the same manoeuvre, in which that officer altogether failed, and then Sir Hussey again spoke of how "Major Anderson and the 50th had performed his wishes without the slightest hint or hesitation." I have mentioned this at length, because it was much talked of at the time, and I was really proud of the opinion of so able and distinguished an officer, and because, as I shall hereafter show, this trifle led to much good to me some years afterwards.

CHAPTER 18

To New South Wales

I was detached with four companies to Maryborough: soon afterwards the well-known priest, the Rev. Dr. Doyle, visited the place, and on the Saturday of his arrival it was publicly announced that he would preach in the Catholic chapel. Being a very celebrated and popular preacher, many of the Protestant inhabitants attended; the church was crowded beyond comfort and standing-room, and all waited past the appointed hour with anxiety and impatience. At last he appeared in front of the altar in his full white robes, and, fronting the congregation, stared fiercely and wildly all around the assembled crowd; he then took off his biretta and threw it violently at his feet, and with his right arm stretched out and his fist clenched he shouted: "I have not come to preach to you, you midnight assassins, you skull-crackers! I am come to tell you that the hand of God is suspended over you, and that you shall not know the end thereof, until you are swept from the face of this earth and open your eyes in hell!"

The congregation moaned and crossed themselves again and again; there followed endless sobs and lamentation, then a dead silence for a minute or two. The Rev. Father now roused himself again and said (pointing to me),"There is the officer commanding the troops, he has got the King's commission in his pocket; and" (turning round to another part of the gallery) "there is the officer commanding the police, he has got the Lord-Lieutenant's commission in his pocket; and I have got" (slapping his hand violently on his side) "the seal of Christ in my pocket. You midnight assassins, go and repent of your sins, while you have yet time." He then retired, and the congregation broke up moaning and crossing themselves as before, and my dear wife and I were truly glad to escape without further fear of molestation. The cholera was raging at this time, and such was the terror occasioned amongst the lower classes by the Rev. Father's denunciation that it was said the deaths from cholera were more than usual for some time afterwards.

We returned to Birr barracks after this, leaving a strong detachment still at Maryborough, and early in April a letter was received by our commanding officer to hold the regiment in readiness to embark for New South Wales. In our service to King and country we had thus far experienced much and suffered much, and now we were to be of further service to England and the Crown in that farthest most outpost of our glorious Empire.

A Brief History of Joseph Anderson's Campaigns

by Eric Sheppard

Publisher's Note

The following passages from Eric Sheppard's book *A Short History of the British Army to 1914* commence in 1801 with the campaign in Egypt and give a background to the period that coincided with Joseph Anderson's early career as a soldier. Although Anderson was not present in this campaign, its history provides the foundation for what followed in Italy and, once again, in Egypt where Anderson played the small part featured in this memoir. This period followed a disastrous campaign for the Allies in the Low Countries.

As this narrative begins, Napoleon's star was still in the ascendant throughout his empire.

The Leonaur Editors

The Campaign in Egypt

Unfortunately the ill-fortune that had pursued the Allies in Holland also attended their efforts in other theatres of war. The French, though they were unable to recover Italy, managed, thanks to dissensions among the Allies, to retrieve their disasters in Switzerland and Germany; suspicion and ill-will first between Russia and Austria, then between Russia and England, widened into positive alienation and finally into a definite breach. Before the campaign of 1800 opened the Second Coalition had been dissolved, and England and Austria were left alone in face of France, now being reorganised and strengthened under the firm and masterly leadership of Napoleon Bonaparte, who had returned from Egypt to effect a coup d'etat, and assume supreme control of the country with the title of First Consul. He at once took the field in person, and in the decisive campaign of Marengo compelled Austria to relinquish her hold of the whole of southern and the greater part of northern Italy. By October she had been compelled to ask for a cessation of hostilities, while Russia, now become an active foe to Britain, was striving to combine the northern Powers of Europe against her former ally.

Meanwhile, the English army, which might have been advantageously utilised in the Mediterranean to assist its ally's operations in Italy, was wasting its energies in a series of petty and futile expeditions. The first of these, directed against Belleisle, off the French coast, was still-born;

and it was not till the middle of June, when the fate of Italy had already been decided at Marengo, that the British Government were in a position effectively to operate in the Mediterranean. Then a policy of raiding Spanish ports found favour in the eyes of ministers, and was only abandoned after two fiascos at Ferrol and Cadiz; so that at the end of the year they had on the credit side nothing to show for all their efforts but the capture of Malta.

A new plan of operations, however, had now been adopted by the Government, which decided to use its Mediterranean army in conjunction with the Turks for the reconquest of Egypt. The forces left in that country by Napoleon, though believed to be in a bad state of morale, were numerically respectable, amounting in all to some 25,000. To deal with these Abercromby was given only 16,000, deficient as usual of many of the essentials of life in the field, and to make up the shortage reliance was placed on a Turkish contingent and a force to be sent from India to the Red Sea, both of which only arrived after the work was practically done. Fortunately for the British, they found powerful allies in the incapacity of the French commander, Menou, and the half-heartedness and lack of staying power of his army.

The French general, though he had ample warning of the British approach to the Egyptian coast about Aboukir Bay, allowed his adversary to reconnoitre his point of disembarkation at his leisure, make thorough-going and lengthy preparations for this very difficult operation, and finally set on shore on an open beach forces which sufficed to drive back the small detachment left alone and unsupported to oppose them. Even so the disembarkation was a daring enterprise which only succeeded thanks to the care and skill of Abercromby and his officers in planning and rehearsing it, and the courage and dash of the troops. Three days later the army moved on Alexandria, driving the still unsupported enemy detachment before it, but halted in face of the hostile main line of resistance, just east of Alexandria, where it proceeded to take up position. Here it had to undergo the counter offensive of the main French army, which Menou had at last brought up from the interior of the country; but he still for some reason neglected to concentrate the whole of the forces at his disposal, so that the disparity of numbers between the adversaries was negligible. All his attacks, which took place mainly against the British right and right centre, were steadfastly met and repulsed, and towards evening he drew off his defeated army to Alexandria. Unhappily Abercromby, the honourable and competent commander, who had been the soul of the campaign, was severely wounded on the field and died a few days later. Hutchinson, who succeeded him, found that so well had the work been begun there was little left for him to do but to reap the fruits of victory.

The French army was dispersed and disheartened; a Turkish column had come to strengthen their enemies, and was moving on Cairo from the north-east, while a force from India under Baird was' about to land on the western shore of the Red Sea with the same objective. Thither also Hutchinson, after investing Alexandria, marched with the main body of his army; weak detachments only opposed him, and by the end of June he had effected a junction with the Turks before the walls of the city, and the French commander was induced to sign a convention under which his troops were to evacuate the country and be transported home to France. Two months later Menou in Alexandria capitulated on the same terms. Baird's force, after a difficult and toilsome march across the whole breadth of the country, arrived just too late for the final operations, which rounded off with brilliance and completeness the victorious Egyptian campaign of 1801.

The Italian Campaign

A force of 7000 under Craig was sent to south Italy to co-operate with a Russian force and the Neapolitan army, with the ultimate purpose of assisting the Austrians in their struggle with the French in north Italy. Here, again, the same fiasco was repeated; the Allies took up a position on the northern frontier of Naples, where they remained until Austria was defeated and compelled to sue for terms, and thereupon hurriedly marched off to the coast and sailed away—the British, however, only as far as Sicily, which they thus managed to save from the wreck of the kingdom of Naples. As it happened, however, Napoleon's uncertainty as to the exact object of this expedition was the determining cause of his strict orders to Villeneuve to leave Cadiz and intercept it—orders which sent the fleets of France and Spain to their final disaster at Trafalgar.

Meanwhile a new ministry had assumed office at home, and the War Minister, Windham, at once set to work to increase the strength of the army by new methods. He reverted to the system of voluntary short service for overseas; took measures to raise by ballot a contingent of 200,000 militiamen, whom he intended later to draft into regular battalions, carried out a drastic reduction of the volunteers, and took some preliminary measures for a levee en masse in case of invasion. The strength of the regular army at home amounted early in 1806 to some 90,000 men, and one effect of Windham's measures was to liberate a large part of this force for offensive operations. Unhappily in the matters of the choice of objectives and the general conduct of the war, the new Government followed all too faithfully in the footsteps of its predecessors.

The British army in Sicily, having evacuated the mainland of Naples before the advance of a French army of invasion in June 1806, embarked on an enterprise for its recovery. Although much hampered throughout his operations by the vanity and incapacity of his naval colleague Sidney Smith, Stuart, who had replaced Craig, effected a landing on the Calabrian coast, and, moving inland, met and defeated the French, who were superior to him in numbers, in a brilliant little action at Maida. The moral effect of this victory throughout Europe, though great and widespread, was somewhat diminished by Stuart's failure to follow up his success, and his return to Sicily consequent on a violent quarrel with the admiral; the French were thus enabled to reoccupy the lost territory at their leisure, and such damage as their prestige had suffered was more than repaired by the rapid and complete overthrow of Prussia, who had at last mustered up courage to defy Napoleon, at Jena, and the occupation of her territory by the victorious Grand Army. From Berlin Napoleon issued the famous Decrees, the first step in his attempt to cripple England by closing against her commerce all the ports of continental Europe.

Meanwhile the latter was left to reap what comfort she might from the success of a little expedition under Baird, which for the second time in ten years conquered the Dutch colony of the Cape of Good Hope. This led directly to perhaps the most ill conceived and criminally foolish military enterprise ever undertaken by British arms—the South American adventure.

This design of crippling Spain by raising a revolution in her American colonies with the help of a joint expedition originated in the fertile brain of Home Popham, the commander of the fleet which had escorted Baird to the Cape, and he persuaded that officer to allow him a battalion under Beresford for the purpose of a descent on Buenos Ayres. As it turned out, the operation was carried out successfully, and for close on two months the tiny force actually remained in possession of the city. The Spaniards then recovered themselves, surrounded it on all sides and forced it to lay down its arms, but not before exaggerated reports of the initial advantage gained had induced the Government not only to despatch reinforcements under Auchmuty for the further prosecution of the campaign, but also to send out another force under Craufurd to take possession of the whole of Chile and connect with Beresford across the whole 900 miles breadth of the continent—a megalomaniac scheme worthy of Chatham at his worst. However, it was later found necessary to use the whole force, now placed under Whitelocke's command, for the recovery of Buenos Ayres, and accordingly after Auchmuty had brilliantly got possession of Monte Video the army was concentrated there, ferried up the Rio de la Plata and landed some thirty miles east of its objective. A difficult and toilsome march, where food and water were scarce and the administrative arrangements to the last degree faulty, brought it before the west face of the city, and next day it was plunged headlong into the streets in a number bf weak columns, unable to see or assist one another. Disaster ensued, several units surrounded on all sides laid down their arms, and Whitelocke was fortunate to be allowed to evacuate the country in safety under the terms of a convention with the enemy. He was, of course, made the scapegoat for the failure, and cashiered for having failed in an impossible task and chosen the only means left him to extricate his army from a position from which no other escape was possible.

While the British were thus wasting their energies in futile and eccentric directions, Napoleon at the end of 1806 had found his triumphant career in Europe checked by the mud of Poland. Fortunately for him Russia at the same time became embroiled in hostilities against Turkey, and this new factor in the situation led directly to a new experiment in futility undertaken by the British Government, which decided to send a fleet through the Dardanelles and a military force to deny Egypt to the French by occupying and holding Alexandria. Both enterprises proved disastrous failures. 6000 men under Fraser succeeded, indeed, in securing Alexandria, but, pushing farther eastward to consolidate their position by occupying Rosetta, were twice beaten off with loss. An attempt was then made to effect by negotiation what could not be accomplished by arms, and terms were finally signed which in fact secured the object of the expedition—if it can be said to have had one, since the French" had apparently not the least intention of actually attacking Egypt. The forces thus foolishly wasted might well have found more profitable employment in Sicily, where the British garrison, none too large, was neutralised throughout the whole of 1807 and 1808 as regards offensive action, first by an outbreak of mutiny in Malta and then by continued and irreconcilable dissensions between its commanders and the corrupt rulers of Naples, while the French established themselves at leisure on the mainland, and late in 1808 succeeded in securing Capri by a *coup de main* under the noses of the British fleet.

The Peninsular War

It being a vital part of Napoleon's campaign against England to close all the ports of the Continent against her commerce, he proceeded at the end of 1807 to take measures to force Portugal into his system. At the same time he conceived designs upon the independence of Spain, France's ostensible but reluctant ally in the dragooning of Portugal—designs which her corrupt and effete rulers were too stupid to fathom or too pusillanimous to resist. 80,000 French troops moved into Spanish territory, ostensibly to act as support to the force under Junot, which, flanked by Spanish armies, pushed forward at breakneck pace to Lisbon, drove the Government to seek refuge on board the British fleet, and secured the whole country without firing a shot. Meanwhile the criminal folly and insane dissensions of the Spanish royal family led Napoleon to believe that he might safely expel them from the throne, and, by setting up in their stead his brother Joseph, reduce Spain to the position of a vassal state of France. The whole of northern and eastern Spain, from the Pyrenees to Madrid, was occupied by French armies; the strong places in that area were seized by force or fraud by the French commanders; and the miserable Bourbons proved, as had been anticipated, no serious obstacle to the Emperor's designs. Yet, despite the apparent absence of any real spirit of patriotism in Spain, the inefficiency and corruption of her upper and governing classes, and the weakness of her armed forces, the whole country, on the first news of the coup d'etat, flared up into insurrection. Provincial juntas or assemblies were set up, local levies were raised and armed, the army was swollen by a flood of recruits, and war to the knife was proclaimed on all sides against the violators of the country. Moreover, the early operations of these newly raised armies against the French, who were of inferior quality and led by mediocre Generals, and suffered from lack of unity of direction, met with unexpected and important successes; the invaders were held in check in Catalonia and repulsed before the walls of Valencia and Saragossa, while in Andalusia a whole corps was compelled to lay down its arms on very discreditable conditions at Baylen. Only north-west of Madrid in the plains of Leon were the French arms victorious, and so tremendous was the cumulative effect, both material and moral, of these disasters that by the end of August the new King saw himself compelled to flee from his capital after a month's residence and take refuge with his armies behind the Ebro.

Meanwhile emissaries both from Spain and from Portugal, which in its turn had risen against the French, had sought for and obtained promises of substantial assistance from Great Britain. Pursuant to this resolve, an expeditionary force of 14,000 men was prepared and the command of it given in the first place to Sir Arthur Wellesley, a general who had already to his credit a brilliant series of achievements in India, and whom it will be simpler to denote from now onwards by his better-known title of Wellington. His mission was to repel the French from Portugal, and on August 1 he commenced the disembarkation of his force in Mondego Bay, 100 miles north of Lisbon. To oppose him Junot had 25,000 men, but these were much scattered, and in order to gain time for their assembly he threw forward a detachment, which encountered and was driven back by the British in the first action of the war at Rolica. Even with the respite thus secured, the French commander could only get together 13,000 of his troops; with these he moved out from Lisbon, and on August 21 assailed Wellington, who had taken up a position at Vimeiro to cover the landing of further reinforcements. His attacks, delivered against the British centre and left, were disjointed and ill-prepared, and were beaten off in succession; had a counter-offensive been undertaken, as Wellington intended, he must have been thrown off his line of retreat to Lisbon, but at the critical moment two newly appointed British Generals-in-Chief arrived to take over command in turn and temporarily paralysed the victorious army, and left the French leisure to make their escape. None the less, their situation was so precarious that Junot was glad to negotiate for and secure the honourable withdrawal of his army from Portugal under the terms of the Convention of Cintra. Public opinion at home was so enraged at what seemed an impotent conclusion to a brilliant campaign that an inquiry was held, from which Wellington alone of the three commanders concerned emerged with enhanced fame.

While Portugal was thus being lost to Napoleon—never, as it turned out, to be regained—the other French armies remained strictly on the defensive behind the Ebro, leaving the Spanish to muster unmolested in their front. By the end of the summer these numbered close on 150,000 men, with 60,000 more in reserve in the interior, but they were unhappily as inferior in quality as they were formidable numerically. Their discipline, armament and leadership left everything to be desired; they had no General-in-Chief, nor indeed did there exist any united direction of the war as a whole, for the central junta which had been set up at Madrid was not only incapable but was supreme only in name. None the less, plans for a general offensive, in which the British were asked to co-operate, were drawn up by the various commanders, but were still only in the stage of discussion when the face of the war underwent a sudden and entire change owing to the arrival of the French Emperor in person at the head of 200,000 of his veterans.

Napoleon had decided once and for all to finish with the war in Spain before the troubles which he knew to be brewing in Germany and Austria should call for his undivided attention; and his coming heralded the opening of an immediate and irresistible offensive. Early in November he burst through the hostile centre on the Vitoria—Madrid road, and dealing fierce blows to either flank hurled the Spanish left back into the Asturian mountains, broke their right into fragments, and forcing his way over the Guadarrama passes entered Madrid in triumph after less than a month of fighting. The Spanish armies were dispersed to the four winds; all resistance seemed at an end, and the victor was planning a further advance westwards for the conquest of Portugal and southwards into Andalusia when the unexpected appearance of a British army on the flank of his line of communications with France gave an entirely new turn to the whole situation.

The British Government immediately after the recovery of Portugal had decided to send forward into Spain, as requested by their Allies, a force of some 36,000 men under Moore, of which 20,000 were to be detached from the army in Portugal, while the remainder under Baird were to be sent from England by sea to Coruna. Moore was further induced, owing to reports of the bad state of the roads in his zone of operations, to divide his own force into two and send his artillery and guns under Hope by way of Madrid, while he himself moved by Salamanca. The army was thus separated into three columns, with their area of concentration fixed around Burgos, where they would be well placed to co-operate with the Spanish armies on the Ebro. Moore's difficulties, owing to lack of money, supplies and transport, and, above all, the complete absence of any reliable information as to either his allies or adversaries, were such that, although he began his march in the middle of October, it was not till the end of November that he himself reached Salamanca, with Hope and Baird 100 miles away on either flank. Here he first heard of the utter rout of the Spanish armies and the French advance on Madrid, and realising the peril of his position resolved to retire while he might. A few days later, however, as the French appeared to be moving not directly westward against him but southward across his front, he determined to venture on a bold stroke at their communications, which were protected only by Soult's isolated corps in the vicinity of Sahagun. He rightly considered that this move, by bringing the whole French army upon himself, would give an all-important breathing space to his allies, and hoped that he himself might manage to evade Napoleon's enveloping toils. He accordingly concentrated his army against Soult, and was about to attack the latter on Christmas Eve when he heard that Napoleon was on the move from Madrid against his flank and rear. Instantly he drew off, and successfully got clear across the Esla at Benavente just before the arrival of the leading cavalry of the Emperor's column, which had moved at breakneck speed through atrocious weather and over bad mountain roads to intercept him. From now on the French had no recourse but to a direct pursuit, which Napoleon soon decided could safely be entrusted to the reinforced corps of Soult. The British rearguard successfully held off the enemy throughout the whole of the ensuing retreat to Coruna, but the rigours of the winter, the shortage of supplies, and, above all, the fierce pace at which Moore conducted the inarch, all but broke up his army into a disorganised mob. A few days' respite at Coruna, however, restored morale and discipline, and when Soult endeavoured to interrupt the embarkation he was heavily repulsed. This success was marred by the untimely death of Moore himself, who was carried off the field mortally hurt in the moment of victory and buried to the sound of French guns a few hours before the last of his army departed.

No character and career in British military history has been more fiercely discussed than Moore's, and it is no easy task to arrive at a satisfactory verdict on either. He was perhaps the greatest trainer of troops in the history of the British army, on which he left an undying mark for good; but as a leader in the field his promise was—perhaps mainly through ill-fortune—greater than his performance. Prior to his last campaign all his tasks had been thankless and difficult and left him little chance for spectacular work; and though the skill and daring of his stroke against Napoleon's communications are deserving of high praise, and the respite thereby gained for Spain invaluable, his ensuing operations were marred by serious blemishes. On the whole, it seems that Moore's abilities and achievements have of recent years been as unduly exaggerated as they had previously been unfairly depreciated, and that his qualities as a man have tended to inspire in his biographers an excessive admiration for his military talents.

The value of the three months' respite gained by Moore's diversion lay not so much in the reorganisation of the Spanish armies effected during that time as in the uprising throughout both Spain and Portugal of those guerrilla bands which, embodying the true spirit of popular resistance to the invasion, were to render impossibly difficult the task of the French commanders and troops, by preventing intercommunication, hampering movement, impeding supply, and inflicting a ceaseless and steady drain of casualties. For the moment, however, the tide of conquest was hardly checked. During the first months of 1809 the situation in Catalonia was restored and the Spaniards driven back to Tarragona; Saragossa fell after an epic defence; Victor, in the Tagus valley, overthrew the Spanish centre under Cuesta at Medellin, and overran Northern Estremadura; and Soult, leaving Ney to complete the conquest of Galicia, moved south from Coruna, invaded Northern Portugal and stormed the city of Oporto. Meanwhile the British troops around Lisbon, now under Cradock, remained inactive, largely because the home Government were hesitating between a continuance of operations in that theatre and the opening of a new campaign in the south of Spain, and only decided for the former because of the unwillingness of the Junta to permit the landing of British troops at Cadiz.

Thus it was not till May that Wellesley, who had superseded Cradock, found himself ready to commence operations with a force of 25,000 British and some 16,000 Portuguese, who had been rapidly reorganised and made ready for service by Beresford, their new Commander-in-Chief. Faced with the choice of striking either at Soult in Northern Portugal or Victor in Estremadura, he resolved to deal first-with the nearest and most dangerous foe. While Beresford moved to threaten Soult's left in the mountains the main army marched due northward on Oporto along the coast, and, driving in the hostile advanced troops, appeared before the city on May 12. Soult's forces were widely scattered, and he could assemble in face of Wellesley no more than 13,000 men, which should, however, have been able to put up a good resistance; but the British by a daring stroke surprised the passage of the Douro under the noses of their adversaries, and compelled them to a hurried withdrawal. Soult's main line of retreat having been successfully cut by the Portuguese, he was compelled to abandon his artillery and baggage and throw himself into the mountains, through which, after a series of hair-breadth escapes, and at the cost of severe privations and heavy losses, he at length succeeded in making his escape to Galicia.

Portugal thus liberated, Wellesley turned south and east

to attack Victor in conjunction with the Spanish armies under Cuesta in Estremadura, and in La Mancha under Venegas. This co-operation, owing to the intractable and jealous disposition of Cuesta, took long to arrange, but it was at length agreed that he and the British, who together could put into line over 60,000 men against Victor's 20,000, should move on Madrid by the Tagus valley, while Venegas should assist by containing or driving back the enemy forces south of the capital. Grave supply and transport difficulties caused the commencement of operations to be delayed till mid-July, and when the Allied armies at length arrived before Victor's chosen position at Talavera, the favourable opportunity of attacking his isolated corps was lost by Cuestra's dilatoriness. Venegas having completely failed to fulfil his mission, the French were enabled to reinforce Victor, oppose 46,000 men to Cuesta—who had alone resumed the advance on Madrid, the British having been brought to a standstill by lack of supplies—and drive him back in disorder to Talavera. Here on July 27 and 28 there took place one of the most fiercely contested battles of the war, in which the 20,000 British bore the shock of more than double their numbers and victoriously repulsed their repeated assaults, both by night and by day, though at a cost of close on 25 per cent of their strength.

The tactical victory remained with the Allies, and next day the French fell back, having been compelled to detach troops to deal with Venegas, who had at last and too late decided to advance on Madrid. While he was being chased back to the south, Wellesley and Cuesta were also withdrawing by reason of a new and unexpected turn in the situation. A French force of 50,000 men, under Soult, having assembled at Salamanca, was moving south against their left rear and threatened to pin them in between the Tagus and the mountains. To escape this peril they were compelled to fall back in haste and take up a position on the south bank of the river near Almaraz, which Soult felt himself unable to attack. From there at the end of August, Wellesley, once more straitened for supplies, retired to the vicinity of Badajoz, firmly resolved that never again would he be inveigled into joint operations with Spanish armies.

This determination remained unchanged, although on both the British flanks—in Leon and in La Mancha—the Spaniards during the last months of 1809 ventured once more upon an offensive in the open field, with the usual results. The army of La Mancha once more marching rashly on Madrid suffered an utter defeat at Ocana, while the Spanish force in Leon, after some initial success, was also repulsed with loss at Alba de Tormes. Only in Catalonia, where Alvarez' magnificent defence of Gerona held the French armies fast before its walls for seven long months, did success smile on the Spanish arms. Moreover, Napoleon, having overthrown Austria and compelled her not only to make peace but to give him a wife from the Imperial House, was now free to reinforce his armies in the Peninsula to almost any extent, and in fact by the beginning of 1810 the French troops in Spain had been increased to close on 300,000 men. By that time Wellington, in expectation that the enemy's next attack would be against Portugal, had transferred his army northwards from Badajoz to a line running from the Tagus at Abrantes to the Mondego valley west of Ciudad Rodrigo.

The hostile offensive, however, was not to develop for some months yet, and the early part of the year 1810 was devoted to a French attack in force on Andalusia. In a rapid campaign Soult overran the whole province to the gates of Cadiz, where the remnants of the Spanish forces, assisted by a British contingent under Graham and the Allied fleets succeeded in maintaining themselves. Here, as elsewhere, invaders were constantly worried by guerrilla bands and partisan leaders. In the north and east of Spain the operations during the course of 1810 resulted less favourably for the French arms. Suchet held down Aragon, but was unable till the autumn to undertake anything outside the borders of that province; while the Catalonian rising was maintained in full flame and kept busy a large army, first under Augereau and then under Macdonald, which was not in a position to undertake any important operation till the end of the year, when siege was at length laid to Tortosa.

Meanwhile the three army corps of the Army of Portugal, 86,000 strong, under Massena, one of the ablest and most experienced of Napoleon's Marshals, began to assemble on the north-eastern frontier of Portugal from March onwards. It was not till June, however, that they were ready to commence active operations, and Wellington utilised to the full the breathing space thus granted him to perfect his measures for the defence of the country. The militia, numbering some 45,000 men, as well as the popular levee en masse, was called out; arrangements were made for the systematic evacuation of the whole area over which the enemy were likely to advance; and the construction of a vast entrenched camp covering Lisbon was completed. This camp, known as the lines of Torres Vedras, comprised two lines of works on a front of 25 miles from the Lower Tagus to the sea, and about 25 miles north of Lisbon, together with a third line close to that city intended to cover the embarkation of the army should this be necessary. The fortifications were as complete as time and labour could make them and their existence remained to the last entirely unsuspected by the French. Meanwhile the Allied army of 60,000 men, of whom about half were British, were held ready in the upper Mondego valley. Hill's Second Division was detached in the Tagus valley to watch for any hostile advance in that quarter, while Craufurd's Light Division, east of the Coa, covered the front of the main body.

In June, Massena laid siege to the frontier fortress of Ciudad Rodrigo, and on its surrender, after a gallant defence of five weeks, assailed Craufurd on the Coa, forced him back over that river after a smart combat, and invested Almeida. The resistance of that place was cut short owing to the explosion of the magazine, which wrecked the town and left the governor with no choice but to capitulate, and after a further three weeks had been passed by the French in collecting supplies all was at last ready for the great offensive. Wellington, relieved of his fears of a simultaneous advance north and south of the Tagus, now drew in Hill to the main army, and was soon notified that Massena had chosen for the march of his 65,000 men what he described as "the worst road in Portugal"—that along the north bank of the Mondego to Coimbra. He at once concentrated his forces to fight, and on September 27 the French found their progress blocked by the whole British army arrayed for battle on the ridge of Bussaco. Their attacks, delivered in succession at two different points two miles apart, were beaten back with considerable loss, and the French Marshal realised that the enemy must be manoeuvred out of his position. He accordingly moved his whole army across a mountain path beyond the left flank of Wellington, who thereupon executed a deliberate and unhurried retirement, by Coimbra, to the lines of Torres Vedras. Massena followed under great difficulties; supplies were short, and hostile militia and guerrilla bands infested his flanks and rear, cut his communications and captured his hospital and depot at Coimbra as soon as he had left that place. Finally, on October 10, he was brought up short before the lines, which, after careful reconnaissance, he declined to attack. In this he was wise, for Wellington could have opposed to his 55,000 men not only the 20,000 second line troops garrisoning the works, but also 58,000 of the field army, ready to deal with any force which should have broken its way through the defences. The French Marshal, with a stubborn resolution exceeding his adversary's expectations, maintained his position under ever-increasing difficulties for a whole month, and then only fell back some 25 miles to a strong position around Santarem, which Wellington in his turn felt but dared not attack.

In this situation of apparent stalemate the campaign of 1810 closed. But the true advantage lay with the British; the French had made their last and greatest effort against Portugal and had failed to achieve their object, and Wellington and his armies had set out on the first stage of that advance which, after many vicissitudes, several checks and more than one set-back, was in the end to carry them forward into France to attend the final obsequies of Napoleon's Empire.

The new phase of the war, that opened with Massena's withdrawal from Portugal, was in its actual results indecisive, leaving the two contending armies at the end in much the same position as at the beginning of the period. None the less the initiative had passed to Wellington, and his adversaries were, for practically the whole of the two years, reduced to a defensive attitude, and compelled to await and parry blows in place of themselves delivering them. On the whole—at least to outward seeming—they were successful in maintaining their positions intact, but the resulting attrition of their armies was so great, and the strain on their resources so increasingly intense, as to leave them in no situation to withstand the powerful British offensive of 1813 and 1814.

The general situation in the Peninsula at the beginning of 1811 was as follows: In Catalonia, Suchet had captured Tortosa and was about to besiege Tarragona, the only fortress still holding out in that province. Soult had more or less subdued Andalusia, but was still held up before the walls of Cadiz; while the north and centre of Spain, with the exception of Galicia and part of the northern coast, though still disturbed by irregular bands, might be regarded as French occupied territory. In January, Soult, feeling himself strong enough to carry out his orders to co-operate with Massena, who was still at Santarem, by an advance against the south-eastern frontier of Portugal, moved up to the Guadiana, routed a Spanish army outside Badajoz and secured possession of that important fortress. Even had he been able to push his victorious career farther he would have been too late to assist Massena; but immediately after the fall of the fortress he was forced to retrace his steps by serious news from Andalusia, where the Spaniards were undertaking an advance on Seville—which eventually came to nothing—and a combined force was attempting to raise the siege of Cadiz.

This expedition of 15,000 men, commanded by the Spanish General La Rena, and including 5000 British under Graham, was sent by sea from Cadiz to disembark at Algesiras and Tarifa, and move against the rear of the investing force under Victor. The unnecessary slowness of its advance, however, gave the latter time to draw off the bulk of his troops and fall unexpectedly on the Allied right flank and rear at Barrosa. Graham's men, though caught at a disadvantage, succeeded in beating off the French attack and inflicting serious loss on their enemies; but the failure of the Spaniards to co-operate in or exploit the victory destroyed all confidence between the Allies, who confined themselves to returning tamely to Cadiz at the very moment when Victor was preparing in despair to raze his works and abandon the siege. Soult, therefore, on his return found the situation restored in this quarter also.

In Portugal, however, fortune had turned decisively against the French. Early in March, Massena, whose army, despite the arrival of strong reinforcements, had sunk to less than

50,000 men, and had completely drained the country round Santarem of supplies and foodstuffs, commenced his retirement. He succeeded in slipping away unknown to Wellington and in gaining several marches on him; and even when his adversary realised what was toward he was unable, having only some 46,000 of all ranks at his disposal, to do more than harass the French rearguard under Ney, who conducted a series of brilliant delaying actions between Santarem and the Mondego. Finding the passages of that river blocked by the Portuguese irregulars, Massena turned eastwards short of Coimbra, and, falling back along the south bank of the river, assembled his army at the end of March in the Celorico-Guarda area, intending to move south to the Tagus valley and menace Portugal on a new line of invasion. Shortage of supplies, however, quickly brought his army to a halt, and Wellington, striking at his left flank, headed him off at Sabugal—one of the most brilliant actions fought by the British in the whole course of the war—and compelled him to fall back, uncovering the fortresses of Almeida and Ciudad Rodrigo, and seek safety and rest for his exhausted and discontented army in the Salamanca area.

In less than three weeks, however, the tenacious stubbornness of the old Marshal brought his troops once more forward to the offensive, for the purpose of raising the investment of Almeida, to cover which Wellington took up a position at Fuentes de Onoro with some 37,000 men, against his adversary's 48,000. After a vain attempt to storm the British centre, Massena succeeded in turning and forcing back their right wing, but only to find himself faced with a new battle-front too strong for him to assail. He therefore fell back once more, but his failure was offset by the daring escape of the Almeida garrison, which succeeded, thanks to culpable negligence on the part of its adversaries, in making its way through the line of investment to its own army, after destroying its guns and stores.

Meanwhile important events were taking place in Estremadura. As soon as Wellington was assured of Massena's retreat, he had despatched Beresford with 18,000 men to rescue, Badajoz. That general, too late to accomplish this, none the less defeated at Campo Mayor and drove back over the Guadiana the weak hostile force left behind by Soult to cover the fortress, and began the siege. Unavoidable delays in opening the investment, and avoidable blunders in its conduct, gave Soult time to collect a force of 24,000 men for the relief of the place. Beresford, with his own troops and a reinforcement of 14,000 Spaniards under Blake, delivered at Albuera a battle which, despite Soult's superiority of generalship, was turned into a victory by the magnificent fighting of the British infantry, who left on the field close on 50 per cent of their effective strength. The shattered French army drew back, and Wellington, who, having left in Beira 30,000 men to watch the Army of Portugal, had hastened to Beresford's assistance with 10,000 men, was enabled to resume the siege.

Although the British commander fully realised that he had at his disposal only a short space before the French assembled in superior numbers before him, his conduct of operations against the fortress followed the same lines as, and met with no better fortune than, the earlier ones. Mafmont, who had replaced Massena after Fuentes de Onoro, hurried with great promptitude to join Soult in the raising of the siege, and though Wellington also drew down his own forces from Beira, he even so found himself able to muster only 54,000 men against his adversaries' 60,000. He therefore drew off to a strong position between Elvas and Campo Mayor, and, when the Marshals were once more compelled to separate by want of food and risings in their rear, brought back his army to a rest area extending from north of the Tagus to the Guadiana, from which he could at need assail either Ciudad Rodrigo or Badajoz.

In August he moved once more to Beira, and took up a position to menace the former place. Marmont and Dorsenne, commanding the French Army of the North, which had all the summer been engaged in a vain attempt to subdue the Galician insurgents, advanced rapidly, caught him for once at a disadvantage, and forced him to fall back in haste to Sabugal, where they once more declined to accept the offered battle, and fell back to disperse in due course for subsistence. The British also took up winter quarters extending from Celorico to south of Ciudad Rodrigo, and a brilliant little exploit by Hill's detachment south of the Tagus at Arroyo Molinos put an end to the British operations of 1811.

In the east of Spain, although Macdonald in Catalonia was. engaged for the greater part of the year in the recovery of the fortress of Figueras, which, surprised by the guerrillas in April, held out till August, Suchet, going from success to success, reduced Tarragona, and moving into Valencia defeated Blake at Saguntum, and in January 1812 captured Valencia city and the remnants of the Spanish army. In Andalusia, however, the French suffered a set-back, Victor's expedition against Tarifa at the end of the year being unable to overcome the sturdy resistance of its Anglo-Spanish garrison.

The campaign of 1812 was to see a face put upon events far other from that of the previous year. It opened with two brilliant strokes by the British army against the fortresses of Ciudad Rodrigo and Badajoz, the twin French sally ports on the frontier between Portugal and Spain, which during the past two years had so greatly facilitated the attack of the one country and the defence of the other. Circumstances in June 1812 were favourable for the attack on Rodrigo, before which Wellington had assembled some 50,000 men and a fairly adequate siege train; Marmont's Army of Portugal, which was responsible for its safeguard, had been weakened by a strong detachment despatched by the Emperor's order to assist Suchet in Valencia, and was scattered in widespread cantonments from the Galician border to La Mancha; while the reorganisation of all the French armies in Spain, then in progress, consequent on the growing menace of war with Russia, was bound to militate against any speedy attempt to succour the fortress. When, therefore, the British army, assembled on the Agueda, advanced and completed the investment on January 8, the siege was carried through undisturbed to the final assault, which took place on the twelfth day and was completely successful, though at the cost of somewhat severe losses; indeed news of the opening of the attack on the fortress only reached Marmont four days before its fall, and he so clearly realised the hopelessness of trying to relieve it that he made no attempt even to concentrate his army for that purpose—and that although his whole siege train was within the place and fell into British hands with it.

After some weeks spent in refitting and reprovisioning his new prize, Wellington, at the end of February, moved south against Badajoz; his siege train was sent round by sea, arid the whole of the army marched off with him, the care of the frontier of Beira against Marmorit being left entirely to the Spanish and Portuguese. Soult from Andalusia was hardly likely to be able to collect sufficient forces to relieve the place in face of the 60,000 British now assailing it unless he were joined by Marmont; nevertheless, two detachments under Graham and Hill were pushed out to east and south-east, and drove back the French corps of observation in Estremadura towards the Sierra Morena, and the operations against the fortress itself were pressed with all possible vigour from March 16 onwards. The works were formidable, and the defence resolute and skilful; none the less, the storm could be ordered for April 6. The two main British assaults were beaten off with ghastly loss, but the subsidiary columns broke into the place and compelled its surrender. The greatness of the achievement was marred by the disgraceful scenes of crime and disorder that took place within the city after its fall.

The efforts of the French Marshals to interrupt the siege were half-hearted and failed of all effect. Soult advanced with a weak force, but, finding himself opposed by the covering detachments of Hill and Graham, and seeing no sign of Marmont, who had earlier promised to come to his aid but had since been forbidden to do so by orders from Paris, fell back to restore the situation in Andalusia, which had, as usual, become menacing after his departure. Marmont on his side had raided Beira, scattered the weak forces in his front, and penetrated to Castello Branco, but, being unable to operate against the fortresses owing to the loss of his siege train, was eventually compelled by the advance of the British army from Badajoz against his left flank and rear to retire hurriedly to the Salamanca area, where his army occupied its former cantonments.

Wellington also dispersed his forces for rest and refitment over a broad space from the Douro to beyond the Guadiana, but ordered Hill in Estremadura to attack Almaraz on the Tagus. The successful surprise and destruction of the bridge at that point severed all direct communication between Soult and Marmont, while the simultaneous restoration of the passage at Alcantara shortened by 100 miles the British lateral route across that river, and greatly facilitated their future operations on either side of it.

Meanwhile, Napoleon, having left Paris to take command of his forces against Russia, had entrusted to Joseph, assisted by Jourdan, the task of controlling and co-ordinating the operations of his various mutually jealous and insubordinate commanders in the Peninsula. But before the new Commander-in-Chief had fairly assumed the reins

Wellington was on the move against Marmont. He had arranged for a series of diversions to assist the main operation by distracting the attention of all the French commanders who might be able to assist him; the Army of the North under Caffarelli was to be amused by the Galicians and the guerrillas of Cantabria, aided by a British fleet under Popham operating off the northern coast of Spain; Hill and the Spaniards would give Soult ample employment; and a force was to be sent from Sicily (where, as will be remembered, there was a strong British contingent in garrison, now under Lord William Bentinck) to land on the east coast of Spain and alarm Suchet for the safety of his new conquests. In mid-June Wellington commenced his advance against Marmont's widely scattered army, but instead of pushing forward to defeat it before it could assemble, sat down to invest the forts of Salamanca, the resistance of which delayed him for ten days and caused him to lose a second excellent chance of attacking his enemy, who had rashly pushed forward with part of his army, with superior numbers and at an advantage.

The French Marshal then fell back, followed by his adversary, to the north bank of the Douro between Toro and Valladolid, where a deadlock of a fortnight took place, Marmont awaiting reinforcements from the Army of the North, which, thanks to the successful operations of Popham and his Spanish allies, failed to materialise, Wellington looking vainly for the arrival of the Galicians on the French right and rear, and disturbed to hear that the Sicilian expedition was also hanging fire. At length Marmont assumed the offensive in his turn, and manoeuvring always to turn his enemy's right, forced him to fall back rapidly to the Tormes at Salamanca. Here, on July 22, while striving to extend his left and intensify his menace to the British line of retreat on Ciudad Rodrigo, he spread his army out on so wide a front as to expose it to a counterstroke by Wellington; the battle, which only commenced at 4 P.M., ended by nightfall in the utter defeat of the French.

Clausel, who succeeded the wounded Marshal in command of the beaten remnants, fell back at his utmost speed to the Douro, being unable even to effect a junction with the reinforcements brought up, just too late, from Madrid by Joseph in person. Wellington, following up his victory with less energy than might have been expected, on hearing that his beaten foes were in safety behind the Douro, turned his main body in the direction of the capital, which Joseph, retiring hurriedly before him, was compelled to evacuate without fighting. On August 12 the British effected their triumphal entry amid immense popular enthusiasm.

The consequences of this success were felt from end to end of the Peninsula. Soult saw himself at last compelled, with death in his heart, to raise the siege of Cadiz and abandon his cherished possession of Andalusia; this he safely effected, and by September had united in Valencia with Suchet, who had also been rallied by Joseph and his army. Here, then, was assembled a very strong force which it was determined to use for a counterstroke against Wellington. Suchet, alarmed by the presence in his front not only of strong Spanish forces but of the 8000 British from Sicily who had at last effected their landing at Alicante, was unable to spare any troops from his own army, but a force of 60,000 men was finally set in motion in the direction of Madrid. This was now guarded only by Hill with some 30,000 men, for Wellington with the other half of his army had moved north against Clausel, and having forced him back from the line of Douro to beyond Burgos, was engaged in the siege of that petty fortress with hopelessly inadequate means.

Its resistance was most gallant, and after five assaults had been repulsed the British commander, finding that Clausel had been reinforced by part of the Army of the North and was advancing against him with 50,000 men against his own 35,000, saw himself compelled to raise the blockade and fall back on the road by which he had come. Unable even to hold the line of the Douro in face of the menace to his rear, he sent orders to Hill to leave Madrid and join him on the Tormes, and himself withdrew to that river, where he assembled his whole force of 70,000 men in his old positions around Salamanca. The massed French armies—the Army of Portugal, which had followed him from Burgos, and Soult's and Joseph's troops, who had reoccupied Madrid and pressed on after Hill—numbered 90,000, but, fearing a repetition of Marmont's disaster, they lost the chance of bringing Wellington to battle and allowed him to draw off before their eyes towards Ciudad Rodrigo. The last stages of the British retreat, though unmolested by the enemy, were attended by widespread indiscipline and disorder comparable to those of the retreat to Coruna—and as little excusable. At length, however, the army was dispersed in winter quarters in Central Portugal between the Mondego and the Tagus.

Elsewhere in Spain throughout the year the guerrilla activity had continued unchecked; but the British contingent in Valencia had remained immobile, paralysed by frequent changes of command and quarrels with its allies.

In appearance, then, the campaign of 1812, as that of 1811, had been indecisive, and its close saw the British back in their old quarters in Portugal. None the less great things had in reality been achieved. The French power in Spain had been undermined to its foundations; their hold on Andalusia and the south had been irretrievably lost, and their tenure of all the central parts of the country rendered insecure; while the British army had proved itself not only a defensive but an offensive weapon of the first order, which its commander was fully capable of wielding in either form of war to the fullest possible effect. In a word, the future was for the British arms full of a promise which the next two years were splendidly to redeem.

Napoleon's expedition to Moscow, undertaken with the largest army he had hitherto led into the field, ended, thanks to the stubbornness of the Russian resistance and the rigours of the Russian winter, in one of the most stupendous catastrophes known in the history of modern times, and at the end of the year he was back in Paris, having left the whole of his mighty army dead or captive behind him, and all Central Europe, so long held beneath his heel, simmering with revolt against his dominion. While he was exerting himself in the spring of 1813 to raise another Grand Army, no longer for offence, but for the maintenance of his far-flung Empire, and ordering large contingents to be sent back from the Peninsula to help form the nucleus of the new levies, Prussia had joined Russia in arms against him, and Austria and Sweden were only awaiting a favourable moment to declare themselves on the same side. A new Coalition, more formidable than any of its predecessors, because founded on a widespread revolt of the peoples rather than on the wills of sovereigns and cabinets, now threatened as never before the whole fabric of the Napoleonic system.

For the moment, however, affairs were quiet in the Peninsula, for the Allied armies, fatigued by the exertions and hardships of the Burgos retreat, and much reduced in strength, were in urgent need of a long period of repose. The French, therefore, whose forces had taken up new cantonments from Le Mancha in the south to Leon in the north, were left at leisure to undertake an operation which had long been called for by the obvious necessities of their situation and by reiterated instructions from Paris,—the clearing of the area on either side of the Bayonne—Madrid high road, their main line of communications with

France, from the guerrilla bands infesting it on either flank. The task, however, was infinitely more lengthy and necessitated the employment of far larger forces than had been calculated either at Paris or at Madrid, and eventually all the Army of the North, under Clausel, was at work in Navarre, on the southern side of the road, and the greater part of the Army of Portugal, under Foy, in Biscay, on the northern side. Their operations continued from February to June 1813, and at the end of these four months, though the irregulars had been harried and had lost much ground, they were still at large and unsubdued, while their adversaries were even more worn out by hard marching and fighting with little tangible result to show for it all.

Meanwhile the remaining French armies—those of the Centre (D'Erlon) and South (Gazan) and part of the Army of Portugal (Reille)—were resting quietly in their cantonments, and Wellington was drawing up his plan of campaign, which was to be put into execution in the middle of May. His force of 80,000 men was to advance in two masses, the one from Ciudad Rodrigo on Salamanca, the other from Tras-os-Montes north of the Douro against the line of the Esla. When the French advanced detachments had been driven back from both these areas the whole Allied force was to reunite north of the Douro and move against the French line of communications, the Burgos—Madrid road, opening for itself as it advanced new bases and lines of supply on the northern coast of Spain, and abandoning those with Portugal.

These preliminary movements of the southern force were successfully carried out in accordance with the programme; but a delay in the passage of the Esla by the northern force gave time for the French to assemble some 57,000 men north of Valladolid to oppose any further Allied advance eastwards. Wellington, however, adhered to his original plan of advancing north-eastwards by his left, his army moving in four columns, Giron's Spaniards on the left, Graham and the main body of the army under his own command in the centre, and Hill on the right, by way of Medina de Rio Seco, Palencia and north of Burgos to the upper Ebro.

The French, in view of this constant threat to their right and rear, abandoned in succession Valladolid, Burgos and the line of the Ebro, and fell back along the Madrid—Bayonne main road in the hope of rallying Clausel and Foy before standing to deliver battle. On June 21, however, they were forced to stand and fight in a disadvantageous position at Vitoria, in order to secure time for the withdrawal of their huge convoy of impedimenta. Wellington planned to envelop both their wings with Hill's and Graham's columns, but the latter failed to press his attack home on the decisive flank in time to prevent the escape of the enemy after a creditable resistance.

The material results of the day were, however, immense; all the French artillery, 150 guns, and the whole of their baggage and material were taken, and the beaten army, thrown off its main line of retreat, fell back in great disorder and much demoralised to Pamplona. The two French detached forces which had failed to arrive in time for the battle were fortunate in being able to make their escape and rejoin the main army behind the Bidassoa; Foy skilfully made his way past the northern flank of the British army to Bayonne, and Clausel withdrew by a very roundabout route down the Ebro to Saragossa and thence back into France by Jaca. Wellington, who had made little attempt to exploit his victory, confined himself to driving back the French rearguards from the Pyrenees passes and establishing his main army on and in rear of that range to cover the sieges of the petty fortresses, San Sebastian and Pamplona, the capture of which he regarded as an essential preliminary to any advance into France. And indeed he might well remain content for the present with his masterly operations of the past six weeks, the results of which had been even beyond his highest hopes; not only had they freed the whole of Northern and Central Spain, and hurled down King Joseph's power in ruins, but they had decided Austria, hitherto wavering at the sight of Napoleon's victories over Russia and Prussia in Germany, to throw her sword into the scale on the Allied side.

A painful contrast to the triumphant British campaign in the north of Spain was afforded by the futile series of operations conducted by Murray in the east, against Suchet. After the latter had assumed the offensive in April and been smartly repulsed at Castalla, Wellington instructed his subordinate to undertake an expedition against the French rear in Catalonia, with the double object of favouring an advance by the Spaniards against Valencia, and preventing Suchet from sending any assistance to Joseph.

The latter purpose was certainly achieved, but Murray's hesitation and folly led to a shameful fiasco before Tarragona, and ruined excellent chances of obtaining a valuable local success. After hovering off the Catalonian coast for three weeks and accomplishing nothing, the expedition returned in disgrace to Alicante, where the Spaniards also had failed to take any advantage of the favourable situation resultant on the despatch of large hostile forces to rescue Tarragona, and it was the news of the disasters in the north rather than any activity on the part of the Allies on his own front that eventually caused Suchet in July to commence his withdrawal from the province of Valencia.

Napoleon who, after his victory at Bautzen, at the end of May had concluded a two months' armistice with his adversaries in Germany, had sent Soult to take command against Wellington as soon as he heard of the fatal battle of Vitoria. The Marshal on his arrival set vigorously to work to rearm and refit his broken troops and restore their discipline and morale, and in a fortnight he considered himself in a position to assume the offensive. During this period Graham, who was conducting the siege of San Sebastian, had been beaten off in a first attempt to storm the place, thanks to the gallant defence of the French garrison under Rey, and to the defective arrangements for the assault; and Soult, having no news of Pamplona and fearing it might be in danger, decided to raise the siege by an attack on the British right wing. Of the four corps in which his army was organised, two under Reille and Clausel were to drive the British from Roncesvalles, another, under D'Erlon, to force the Maya Pass, and both columns were then to converge on Pamplona. The fourth corps, Villatte's, was left on the Lower Bidassoa to cover Bayonne against a possible counter-offensive by the Allied left.

On July 25 the British advanced troops were forced back after fierce fighting both from Roncesvalles and from Maya, but whereas D'Erlon's column was unable to make much progress in the Bastan valley beyond the latter pass, the British right retreated with unnecessary precipitation to within 2 miles of Pamplona, where it finally turned to stand at Sorauren.

The French followed up more slowly, and Wellington, who had received tardy information of the danger on this flank, was thus enabled to assemble a force which, though considerably inferior to that of his adversary, proved sufficient to inflict on him a bloody repulse. Soult then planned to withdraw his left wing from before Sorauren, and unite it with D'Erlon's corps for a fresh operation against the Allied centre, but counter-attacked while in the act of executing this perilous manoeuvre, Reille and Clausel were defeated and driven northwards in disorder; part made their escape to St. Jean Pied de Port, the greater part fell back upon D'Erlon, who was compelled to abandon his attack on the British centre and seek safety by the route along the upper Bidassoa. Although harried by the British divisions of the centre and left, and suffering considerable losses in the process, the French main body made its escape to rallying positions on the heights of Vera, only to be unceremoniously hurled from them by the first arriving troops of their pursuers, and compelled to fall back to its old lines in the lower Bidassoa and Nive valleys.

Once more, however, Wellington, ignorant of the state of affairs in Germany and unwilling to undertake such an operation as the invasion of France without thorough preparation, refrained from pressing his advantage, and recommenced the two sieges which had been interrupted by Soult's advance, his army being disposed in its former covering line on the crest of the mountains. While the French were resting and fortifying a defensive position on a long front of 20 miles from the mouth of the Bidassoa by way of Vera and Sarre to Ainhoa, the siege of San Sebastian was being pressed with renewed vigour, and by the end of August all was ready for the delivery of the second assault. It was little better managed, and seemed likely to meet with little better success than the preceding one, when a lucky explosion allowed the stormers to force an entry amid the resulting confusion; and while Rey retired to the castle, which only capitulated after renewed battering a week later, the victorious assailants gave themselves up to an orgy of violence and drunkenness that surpassed even the similar disgraceful scenes at Ciudad Rodrigo and Badajoz.

On the very day of the assault Soult made an attempt to break the investment by pushing his right wing forward over the Bidassoa between Vera and the sea, but his attack was not vigorously pressed and was easily beaten off, the Spaniards bearing the brunt of the combat and acquitting themselves with great credit. Relieved by the fall of San Sebastian of one of his preoccupations, and of another by the news that Austria had joined the Coalition against Napoleon, who would now be prevented by the renewal of hostilities in Germany from detaching any troops to the front in South France, Wellington now determined in his turn to attempt the passage of the Bidassoa. More skilful and more fortunate than his adversary, he successfully established his left wing under Hope on the eastern bank near the mouth of the river, while his left centre under Alten drove back the French from Vera to the Rhune mountain.

Soult's generalship and the fighting spirit of his troops on this day were alike of inferior quality, but once more the British general refrained from pursuing his advance until the fall of Pamplona, which did not take place till the end of October, finally secured his rear. The French had made good use of the opportunity thus afforded them of strengthening their new positions south-west and south of St. Jean de Luz and on the Rhune by the time the Allies attacked on November 10, but their labour was wasted. In the so-called Battle of the Nivelle, where the Allies' 90,000 men were opposed to Soult's 57,000, Wellington demonstrated against the French wings with Hope's and Hill's corps, while his centre under Beresford broke through their centre on the Rhune, and the defenders, abandoning their positions all along the line, retreated to the line of the Nive on either side of Bayonne.

Wellington, following them up, threw Hill's corps over the upper course of that river with a view to turning Soult's left, and by this division of his forces gave the Marshal an opportunity—which he was not slow to seize—of throwing himself with all his forces on a half of the Allied army. However, he profited little in the end from his attacks, which were delivered first against Hope's wing between the lower Nive and the sea and then against Hill on the heights of St. Pierre beyond the river, where the French were with difficulty repulsed in one of the hardest fought encounters of the war.

Bad weather now enforced a pause in the operations, lasting till the end of 1813, during which period both combatants were reduced in numbers, the French by the urgent demands of the Emperor's armies for reinforcements of trained men, the Allies by the refusal of Wellington, who was well aware of the importance, from the point of view of the security of his troops and the success of his future operations, of the necessity of not arousing the hostility of the population, to take with him into France any Spanish troops with a tendency to plunder. Thus, by January 1814, Soult, who could dispose of no more than 48,000 men against his opponent's 80,000, was preparing to abandon Bayonne to its own resources, and to draw off his army to a new line facing south-west behind the Adour and the Gave d'Oloron.

In the east of Spain, Bentinck, who had replaced Murray and was soon in his turn to give way to Clinton, had since July been following up Suchet in his leisurely withdrawal along the coast from Valencia by Tortosa and Tarragona to Barcelona, his advance against the latter city being sharply checked at Ordal. His successor made no further attempt to press his adversary, who by the end of the year had assembled his forces around Gerona, and there halted to await the result of a new diplomatic move by Napoleon. The latter, having suffered a complete defeat at the hands of embattled Europe at Leipzig, had withdrawn the remnants of his army into France, and was there preparing for that magnificent defensive campaign of 1814 which Wellington and many good judges after him considered to be perhaps the finest example of his genius for war. Meanwhile, he had devised a scheme for freeing himself from the menace of Wellington's armies on his southern frontier, and recovering the use of his own troops in that theatre by the signature of the Treaty of Valencay with his prisoner Ferdinand VII., in accordance with the terms of which the latter, in exchange for his restoration to the Spanish throne, engaged to effect the withdrawal of all the contending forces from Spanish territory. This, however, the Cortes, the actual government of Spain, refused to ratify, and, accordingly, Suchet remained in possession of Northern Catalonia until the conclusion of hostilities.

Meanwhile the Allies were preparing to invade France from the east, and Wellington set to work to force Soult's new defensive line. While Hope on the left with the help of the fleet crossed the Adour below Bayonne, and circling round to north and east of that place completed its investment, the main body of the Allies drove the French in succession from the Gave d'Oloron and the Gave de Pau, and attacked them in their chosen battle position at Orthez.

After some vicissitudes the hostile right and centre were beaten from their ground, and the whole forced to retreat hurriedly behind the upper Adour at Aire. From this town Soult determined to effect his further retirement eastwards and south-eastwards along the foot of the Pyrenees so as to divert the Allies from a direct invasion of France, and approach nearer to Suchet's army, which he hoped might thus be induced to come to his assistance. Wellington, after detaching a force to occupy Bordeaux, where the population were eager to revolt against Napoleon and to raise the white flag of the Bourbons, followed up the retreating French army towards Toulouse.

At the beginning of April the Marshal halted once more on the line of the Garonne, and stood to fight around that city. The battle that ensued was decided after several premature and partial efforts by the advance of the main column of attack under Beresford, along the foot of the hills occupied by the French right, and the storming of those heights, and Soult, menaced with investment within the walls, made haste to withdraw his army before it was too late. The battle was needless waste of life on both sides, as was a fruitless sortie by the garrison of Bayonne a few days later; for the armies of the Coalition had already, after many set-backs, forced their way into Paris, compelled Napoleon to abdicate the Imperial throne, and put an end alike to the war and to French supremacy in Europe.

Thus the Peninsular War, the mightiest conflict hitherto fought by the British army, ended in a blaze of glory. During its course, to use Napier's words, England " expended more than one hundred million sterling on her own operations; she subsidised both Spain and Portugal, and with her supplies of clothing, arms and ammunition, maintained the armies of each, even to the guerrillas. From 30,000 to 70,000 British troops were employed by her; and while her naval forces harassed the French with descents upon the coasts, and supplied the Spaniards with arms and stores and money after every defeat, her land forces fought and won nineteen pitched battles and innumerable combats, made or sustained ten sieges, twice expelled the French from Portugal, preserved Alicante, Cartagena, Tarifa, Cadiz, Lisbon; they killed, wounded and took 200,000 enemies, and the bones of 40,000 British soldiers lie scattered on the plains and mountains of the Peninsula. For Portugal she reorganised a native army and supplied officers who led it to victory; and to the whole Peninsula she gave a General whose like has seldom gone forth to conquer."

The West Indies

In the West Indies the British, despite the usual serious drain of disease, secured their position by the capture, in a series of well-conducted operations, of the French strongholds of Martinique and Guadeloupe and of the Dutch islands, thus establishing their supremacy throughout the Caribbean Sea. In the East an attempt was made in 1803 to complete the occupation of the island of Ceylon, the coastal parts of which, as has been narrated, had been conquered from the Dutch during the war with the French Revolution. The interior of the island was overrun with little resistance, and the Cingalese capital of Kandy was garrisoned by a small force of troops; some months later, however, these were beleaguered and induced to capitulate and treacherously massacred, and no attempt was made for the time being to avenge them. As some compensation for this disaster in the East Indies, Mauritius and Bourbon fell into the hands of a British expedition from India in the course of the year 1810, and in the following year a force of 12,000 men under Auchmuty landed on the Dutch island of Java, garrisoned by 20,000 good troops, stormed the enemy's strong and well-fortified entrenched camp in the face of a two to one superiority, and compelled a capitulation after a six weeks' campaign—one of the most brilliant little affairs of its kind in the history of the British army.

ALSO FROM LEONAUR
AVAILABLE IN SOFTCOVER OR HARDCOVER WITH DUST JACKET

CAPTAIN OF THE 95th (Rifles) *by Jonathan Leach*—An officer of Wellington's Sharpshooters during the Peninsular, South of France and Waterloo Campaigns of the Napoleonic Wars.

THE KHAKEE RESSALAH *by Robert Henry Wallace Dunlop*—Service & adventure with the Meerut volunteer horse during the Indian mutiny 1857-1858

BUGLER AND OFFICER OF THE RIFLES *by William Green & Harry Smith* With the 95th (Rifles) during the Peninsular & Waterloo Campaigns of the Napoleonic Wars

BAYONETS, BUGLES AND BONNETS *by James 'Thomas' Todd*—Experiences of hard soldiering with the 71st Foot - the Highland Light Infantry - through many battles of the Napoleonic wars including the Peninsular & Waterloo Campaigns

A NORFOLK SOLDIER IN THE FIRST SIKH WAR *by J W Baldwin*—Experiences of a private of H.M. 9th Regiment of Foot in the battles for the Punjab, India 1845-46

A CAVALRY OFFICER DURING THE SEPOY REVOLT *by A.R.D. Mackenzie*—Experiences with the 3rd Bengal Light Cavalry, the Guides and Sikh Irregular Cavalry from the outbreak to Delhi and Lucknow

THE ADVENTURES OF A LIGHT DRAGOON *by George Farmer & G.R. Gleig*—A cavalryman during the Peninsular & Waterloo Campaigns, in captivity & at the siege of Bhurtpore, India

THE COMPLEAT RIFLEMAN HARRIS *by Benjamin Harris as told to & transcribed by Captain Henry Curling*—The adventures of a soldier of the 95th (Rifles) during the Peninsular Campaign of the Napoleonic Wars

THE RED DRAGOON *by W.J. Adams*—With the 7th Dragoon Guards in the Cape of Good Hope against the Boers & the Kaffir tribes during the 'war of the axe' 1843-48

THE LIFE OF THE REAL BRIGADIER GERARD - Volume 1 - THE YOUNG HUSSAR 1782 - 1807 *by Jean-Baptiste De Marbot*—A French Cavalryman Of the Napoleonic Wars at Marengo, Austerlitz, Jena, Eylau & Friedland

THE LIFE OF THE REAL BRIGADIER GERARD Volume 2 IMPERIAL AIDE-DE-CAMP 1807 - 1811 *by Jean-Baptiste De Marbot*—A French Cavalryman of the Napoleonic Wars at Saragossa, Landshut, Eckmuhl, Ratisbon, Aspern-Essling, Wagram, Busaco & Torres Vedras

AVAILABLE ONLINE AT
www.leonaur.com
AND OTHER GOOD BOOK STORES

www.ingramcontent.com/pod-product-compliance
Lightning Source LLC
Chambersburg PA
CBHW021003090426
42738CB00007B/630